Learner Services

Please return
on or before
the last date
stamped below

**CITY COLLEGE
NORWICH**

KT-418-715

A FINE WILL BE CHARGED FOR OVERDUE ITEMS   OLLEGE

Bright Pen

	233-15
Class	796.334 SEE
Cat.	SSA	Proc	3wL

Visit us online at:
www.authorsonline.co.uk

233 395

A Bright Pen Book

Copyright Richard Seedhouse © 2007

Cover design by Ty Power © 2007

England Women and FA Women's Premier League Photographs
supplied by James Prickett. www.jamesprickett.co.uk

Book layout and diagram designs by Ty Power.

All other photographs courtesy of Coundon Court Football Club
its players, parents and coaches.

ISBN 978-0-755210-74-9
Authors OnLine Ltd
19 The Cinques
Gamlingay, Sandy
Bedfordshire SG19 3NU
England

Note: While every effort has been made to ensure the technical accuracy of the content of this book,
neither the author nor publishers can accept any responsibility for any injury or loss sustained as a result of
the use of this material.

This book is also available in e-book format, details of which are available at
www.authorsonline.co.uk

Contents

Acknowledgements

The writing and publishing of this book has been a long and testing journey into the unknown and I would never have reached the end if it were not for some very special friends and family. I would like to take this opportunity to thank them all for their belief in me and support in making this book a reality. In particular Barry Morris, Roger Seedhouse, Roger Willis, Terry Harvey, Michelle Hickmott and David Seedhouse. Their ideas, help in proof reading, photography and editing of the final book is much appreciated. I would also like to thank Ty Power for his wonderful diagrams and valued input particularly into the covers, design and layout of the finished book. Richard Fitt of Authors Online www.authorsonline.co.uk also deserves massive thanks for his constant reassurance and guidance. I would also like to thank James Prickett www.jamesprickett.co.uk for the use of his great action photographs. Special thanks also need to go to everyone involved with Coundon Court FC especially Sam White and John Hooke. I would also like to take this opportunity to thank Birmingham County FA and in particular Tom Stack and Natalie Justice for thier help and support in my development as a coach. Most of all I would like to thank my long-suffering family particularly my wife, Kirsten. Your love, friendship and support has enabled me to turn my dreams into reality and I thank you.

For 'Luke'

Introduction

This book is broken down into eleven chapters. We will begin with a very basic warm up and continually progress through the basic football skills onto games and finish by preparing session plans. Each skill will be discussed and coached through a series of drills.

The intention of this book is to stimulate the reader to interact through questions. It is also intended to provide the coach with the knowledge and ability to better use other coaching books or drills.

As you go through the chapters you will be questioned. These will refer to what, how and why you can use the drill to coach. The questions will appear in bold type and are a time to think and reflect on an answer.

You will be asked to think about how your players might cope with the drills.

How will they perform? What can you improve? How can you coach?

You may want to read the book with a notebook and pen handy. You can then jot down your own thoughts and answers to the many questions. You can expand upon the drills and invent variations or even new drills and try them out on the training field. The aim is to challenge you as a coach to think about what you coach and how.

The first drill in each chapter will always be the easiest. As will the first chapter. We will go from a very basic understanding of a warm up through to quite complex drills in the later chapters. We will also look at the different skill levels or ages of players and their requirements and limitations. Learn how the same drill can be adapted from the young beginner to the older or more experienced player. We will progress all the drills within each chapter logically with the progressions becoming increasingly more difficult.

As we go through the various chapters we will look at the different styles of coaching. All players learn differently so we have to adapt our coaching methods so they can understand and learn.

We will look at how questioning your players about a drill will make them think about their own technique. You may as the coach have to guide them to the correct solution. In some cases you may need to clearly explain what is required. A picture is worth a thousand words so demonstrate what you want. A demonstration cuts the waffle of an explanation.

The manner in which you coach is crucial. Think about the age of your players and the way you interact with them. Barking commands and getting annoyed with 6 year olds because they cannot do a Cryuff turn will not improve them. Gently build your players confidence through small successes and challenge them to take the next step, but most of all be patient.

We will also look at introducing fun to the session. When the players are enjoying themselves they are much more likely to listen. They will be relaxed and willing to learn, or try out new things to improve and gain an edge over their peers. If they are having fun they are less likely to worry about the cold or the rain. So by creating a fun relaxed coaching session we are actually creating a better atmosphere for our players to learn and be coached.

The final objective of this book is for all new parents and coaches to realise that education is key to coaching. This book gives you an insight into the many different coaching points and topics. It also provides you with some of the ways and means to coach these points. I hope this book will show you that coaching is more than setting out a drill. I hope it triggers a spark to learn more. There are many coaching courses, which can and should be taken. This book is written to compliment these courses, which will provide you with further information and details to coach your players correctly.

*Coaching*the*Coach* -
Warm Up

Warm Up

Warm Up

Did every training session you were ever involved with or see start with a warm up? Should every session start with a warm up? The players may ask you to explain why we need to warm up, what are the benefits?

So, why do we need to warm up?

We warm up to prepare the body for the activity ahead. This means raising the heart rate to pump blood and oxygen to the muscles. This in turn means the muscles can be stretched safely and primed for movement. The warm up should start slowly and increase in momentum to game speed. This gives the muscles the chance to stretch lightly at first.

The warm up also acts to stimulate the minds of the players and get them mentally prepared for the rest of the coaching session.

So now we understand why we have to warm up at the beginning of a coaching session.

We will start this particular warm up with all of our players jogging around within a 20x20 yard coned square.

We will begin with the very basics. Make sure the players stay within the square at all times. This is especially important for our younger players. It means we can keep them all in one place and safely under control. Remember while the players are at your coaching session, they are your responsibility.

So what else can we do without the ball?

We can start as previously stated with light jogging forwards and backwards.

We can introduce skipping. When skipping promote turning the ankle upward so the player's toes point 90 degrees up into the air. This will help stretch the calf muscles. We can also encourage our players to swing their arms forwards and backwards.

The players can continue jogging on their toes but incorporate knee lifts. The players should alternate bringing their right and left knees straight up to touch their hands. Their hands should be in front of them at hip level with their palms facing the ground. This will stretch the back of the players bottom and work the quads and calf muscles.

We can also have the players alternate bringing their right and left legs up backwards, so the heel of the foot kicks the player's bottom. This will stretch the top of the player's thigh or quadriceps and work the hamstrings.

Whilst jogging our players can alternately bring their knee up and across their body. The right knee is brought up to touch the left elbow, which is lowered, and vice versa. This will further stretch the hip and lower back and work the quads.

We can include two footed jumps off the floor. The players should point their toes at the ground when they jump, as it will work the ankle and calf muscles.

We should also stretch the groin. We can do this by pretending to step over a gate, which is to the side of the player. The player should bring their left knee straight up in front of them keeping their leg bent 90 degrees at the knee. They can then open their leg turning it out to the left. They should repeat the dynamic stretch with their right leg bringing it up and turning it out to the right.

We need to incorporate movements that will be used in the game ahead. These will prime the muscles that will be needed during the training session.

Players can simulate kicking the ball using left and right feet. They should kick the right foot high up and across their body. The right foot should finish high in front of the left shoulder and vice versa. This will stretch the hamstrings.

These are all very basic movements, which I am sure you have all seen, and know.

But how can we mentally prepare our players, what can we do to make our players think?

Split the players into pairs and number them 1 and 2. The number 1 is the leader and moves about the square using any of the warm up movements we have seen so far. Number 2 then follows and copies the actions of number 1, be it skipping, jumping, jogging, knees etc. Can your players think of new movements? Ask them and remember to switch the leader so both players have to think and improvise.

How does this prepare our players?

Firstly the leader will need to concentrate on what the warm up movements are. This will help them remember the moves. Secondly they need to think of which one to use, when to change and to which one. The follower will need to concentrate and keep up with the changing movements of the leader.

Here is another idea which can be used at any time during the warm up or whole session. While the players are jogging about how about shouting a number and the players have to stop everything and get into groups of that number as quickly as possible. They do not have to be exact groups as any left over players could be deemed to have lost.

What can we do to add some fun?

How about a game of cones?

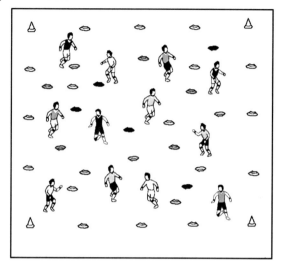

We split our players into four teams and position each team on a corner of the square. Each team is given a colour, which matches the colour of a set of five cones (disc markers) placed randomly within the square. So in the diagram above we have five black, five dark grey, five light grey and five white cones. We also have four teams of three players. The teams being the black, dark grey, light grey and white. Obviously you will use red, blue, yellow or orange cones and bibs for your session. On the coach's command the players from the teams run around in the square trying to turn over all the other teams cones and stand their own up properly. After a set time, 30 seconds or a minute, the coach finishes the drill and the team with the least cones overturned wins. This drill promotes concentration, awareness, and physical preparation for the session ahead.

Another example of a warm up game is the simple game of tig or tag. This is a simple chasing game where you pick one player to be "on" or "It". They then have to run about inside the 20x20 yard square trying to catch any of the other players to "tag" them and pass on the being "it" responsibility of running around and "tagging" another player. To increase participation you can have a number of players being "it".

We now have to adapt the rules so that when a player is tagged they have to stand still with their arms out. Any other player who has not been tagged can then free them by running under their outstretched arms. Play for a couple of minutes and then switch the players who are "it".

This game, like the cones game is a great drill for speeding up the warm up and getting the players up to match speed. It also gets the joints and muscles fully stretched as players weave and dodge about trying to avoid being "Tagged" or overturn cones.

Lets now introduce footballs to our warm up.

With our players back in pairs give one of them a ball. This player is the server. If you have an odd number simply have one group of three. The server performs a throw in to their partner who then passes the ball back to them. The player or receiver can then move off to find another free server and perform the same throw in and pass back routine. For young players you may want to use an underarm throw, as it will be more accurate.

How many different ways can we pass the ball back to the server?

1. Volley pass, promote contact with laces of the boot and remember to make use of both feet.
2. Side foot volley; promote contact with the instep of the foot.
3. A simple header, contact with forehead and eyes open.

I am sure you can think of many more including combinations, the chest then instep for example.

As we go through the book you will find many of the drills shown can be incorporated into the warm up.

It is also a good idea to promote ball familiarity, lots of quick passing or ball juggling. Towards the end of the warm up is also a great time to practice technical turns, as the players are fresh and mentally prepared to learn.

This is a brief insight into the very basics of a warm up. You should watch qualified coaches and look at their warm up routines. Maybe you can use some of their drills and ideas. The important thing to remember is why we warm up and therefore does the drill or game fit the objective.

*Coaching*the***Coach* -
Dribbling

Dribbling

Dribbling I – Simple Dribbling

This drill involves a squad of players in another 20 x 20 yard coned square. All the players have a ball and begin dribbling around inside the square. This is a great drill as all the players have a ball and yes they are practicing close control and dribbling skills. The drill provides a natural challenge as other players are in the same space. They have to keep their heads up and eyes open so they are aware of the players around them and the edge of the square. But are you coaching them?

Most players will predominantly use only their favoured foot.

What can we do to coach or improve?

Let us add a rule, the players must use the instep of both feet, left then right then left then right and so on. Show the players what you mean by demonstrating dribbling with the instep of both feet. Make sure everyone understands.

How do we know they have understood?

Ask them watch them. Most players use the instep easily so can we challenge them further?

How could we change it?

You could always try speeding them up "How fast can you go"

If you challenge them to speed things up and dribble faster what might happen? Could they revert back to their favourite foot again? Can you see this happening as your players train? If so ask them if they think they are doing anything wrong? How can they improve? Demonstrate dribbling with both feet and show how the ball is always under control. The challenge is using both feet and fast.

What else could we do? How could you change and challenge dribbling with one foot? How about the instep, outside and sole of that foot, let's see if they can do that.

Should they try with both feet?

Of course get the players to try the instep, outside and sole of both the right and left feet. Lets challenge them further, how about the coach shouting, "change" to swap

from right foot to left foot. Explain clearly and maybe ask a player to shout, "change" as you demonstrate.

When dribbling would you have your knees bent slightly and arms out for balance? Yes, then demonstrate and explain.

How can we create a bit of fun?

What if the coach shouts "Both" and then the players can use both feet alternately. If the coach shouts "Left" the players can only use the left foot and "Right" for the right foot and "Sole" for the sole of the foot. Who reacts the quickest? Who has to look round to see what other players are doing?

Now the environment has completely changed. We now have a more challenging use of all parts of both feet, reacting to the coach and with a bit of fun.

Can you think of more "rules" that we could use or a way of making it harder?

We could add "sole forward" and "sole backward" to get them to use the sole of the foot more and also in a direction.

We can give each "Rule" a number then the players have to engage the brain to remember which rule relates to which number i.e. 1 is Left foot, 2 is right foot, 3 is sole and so on.

What if we allocate each rule a colour and the coach has three coloured cones if they raise the red cone then the player has to use the left foot, blue cone right foot and a yellow cone signifies the sole. This means the players have to dribble about but keep their heads up watching the coach to see which coloured cone they have raised.

Remember to base these progressions on the skill and age levels of your players. Begin basically with one command and introduce more complications slowly and gently. With younger players these progressions could continue over several sessions. Older players may go straight to the more complicated drills. Why? If you give them a drill, which is not demanding enough or too easy they will lose interest and confidence in you as a coach.

Would holding up cones and raising the dribbling players head help a player in a game?

Of course, the more comfortable a player can be dribbling with the ball at their feet the better. This makes it easier for them to look up and see the players and opposition around them and where a pass can be played.

Would it be good to observe the players from the middle or the outside of the coned square?

I think you will agree that if you stand in the middle of the square you could also get in the way. So observing from the outside is far better.

I'm sure you have seen or can think of a few more "rules" that you can introduce to the drill, which you are now actively managing. You are dictating the degree of difficulty dependant upon the skill levels of the players. Introducing progressions and most importantly what and how you coach.

Do not expect a beginners group of 5 year olds to dribble about with the instep and outstep of both feet whilst watching for the coach to hold up a different coloured cone. Why? Because they probably wont even remember which colour relates to which foot.

Dribbling 2 – Dribbling Round the Cones

Now we will move onto a more formal yet standard drill. Everyone has seen a line of players staring out at a line of four or five cones spaced a foot or so apart. The first player in the line has the ball at their feet. On the coach's command the first player proceeds to dribble in and out of the cones and back again to pass to player number two who does the same.

Before we look at our drill let us consider the organisation and another potential problem.

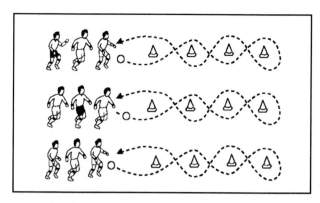

You have set out the drill above for your nine players as shown but unfortunately one of your players does not turn up and you are down to eight, what will you do?

It would be easier if you had the same number of players on each row of cones as they would then start roughly at the same time and finish roughly at the same time. This will make the drill easier to coach as players are not standing about waiting for one person or the odd player to finish, especially difficult if players are young or it is cold.

The first thought is probably to go for four lines of cones with two players on each line. This increases the number of drills being watched from three to four and means the coach has to keep an eye on a wider area but can be done. We could however think laterally, put two players at each end of two lines of cones. This gives the players less waiting time between turns and also means the coach only needs to watch two drills.

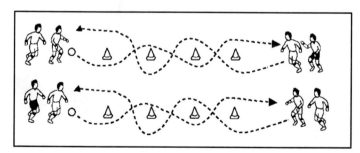

As the coach you will always have to adapt, you may have more or less players or even be a coach short. In these instances we must think about the organisation and how we can tweak the session to adapt to the circumstances.

Now lets get back to the drill and again we can supervise the players as they weave through the cones and yes, they are learning. The drill is helping them to practice close ball control. But can we improve the drill and can we coach?

Watch the younger players, can you spot any problems?

Many younger players will try and run around the ball so they can kick it back in another direction using their favourite foot. As the coach can you stop this and promote the use of both feet?

Can we get them to use the instep of their right foot when they kick left and the instep of the left foot when they kick to the right?

Show them how this makes it easier and faster, demonstrate and explain. Watch them to see if they have understood, did they do it right?

How else could we use this simple drill to improve our dribbling skills or adapt it for better players?

Going back to the warm up rules we have just used we could promote the use of the inside and outside of just the right foot.

Use the instep to kick to the left and the outside to kick back to the right. We could go out using just the right foot and return using the left foot.

How can we create a bit of fun?

Simple, races can be used three goals for finishing 1st, two for 2nd and one for 3rd. Can you get the players waiting involved? Encourage the teams to cheer on their player doing the drill. If you make the cones to dribble round different colours for each of the teams you can name the teams after the colour of their cones. The reds can easily cheer, "Come on Reds".

Have you seen a change in the performance?

Does the pressure and need for a quick time in the race mean that the players have reverted back to using only their favourite foot? If they have, are they going quicker or is the ball going further away from the cone which means they take longer to get around them?

After a race has finished stop them and ask if there were any problems? What will they do next time to go faster or improve? Coach them to concentrate on lots of small touches with both feet, show them it improves their speed. Demonstrate by exaggerating the problem so they can see. Show them the difference in speed.

Can we progress this drill to make it harder or for more accomplished players?

Less space between the cones and more cones are obvious ones but how about moving them to a more zigzag pattern rather than a straight line of cones.

If you have used this drill before or seen it coached by others. Did you adapt? Did you demonstrate? Did you educate or coach your players? Will you do it differently next time and if so how?

Dribbling 3 – Through the Gates

For this we move back to our original 20 x 20 grid but with a series of gates or goals placed within the square. The gates are two cones placed roughly two feet apart. Make sure we have five or six more gates than players.

For the organisation of your grid would you use the same colour cones to mark out the square as the cones you use for the gates?

We could also ask if you would use the same coloured cones for the pair of cones signifying the gate or one blue and one white for example?

The organisation or setting out of your drill is incredibly important and needs to be clear and precise especially for younger players. In this instance we could use white cones to mark out our 20 x 20 square and use pairs of blue cones to signify our gates, if we need more gates then use pairs of red cones, any colour but white.

These details could be the difference between confused players and a well-organised and effective drill.

To begin the drill each player has a ball and tries to dribble through as many gates as possible in a set time e.g. 30 seconds, only one player can go through a gate at a time.

Watch the players and observe the technique. Can you see anything you might want to coach?

Are they using both feet or is this new challenge making them revert back to their trusty favourite foot? Are they standing in a queue waiting for a gate to empty? What will you do?

Ask the players if there are any problems, do they have any suggestions as to how they can improve what they are doing.

Lets explain and demonstrate the advantages of using both the left and right foot again. The ball is always close and under control. Introduce the coaching point and see if they understand and improve. How will you know? Ask them watch them. Once they understand this point we can then progress. Ask them again are there any other problems? Are the players getting their heads up in between touches? No, then lets explain the problems. Bumping into each other or their balls, not knowing which way to go. Coach them to raise their head and look around while dribbling, why? So they can see the players around them and the next available free gate to aim for.

Do they take lots of little touches with the ball always under control or are they taking a big kick toward the next gate and running after it?

If they take a big kick toward the next gate what could be a problem, question your players, do they know?

Another player could take their ball or even kick it away; the ball could go past the gate or even way off target losing more time. Demonstrate the problems.

How could we use this drill for more advanced players?

1. The number of gates could be reduced.
2. The size of the gates could be reduced.
3. Decreasing the size of the square would mean a smaller area to work in and control the ball.
4. Different coloured gates could be used so the players cannot go through the same colour gate in succession.

How can we create some fun?

The players could count how many gates they go through and we could have a winner, most gates after 30 seconds.

Think, with very young inexperienced players would you as the coach pick on a player and ask how many gates they went through or "goals" they scored?

Be careful, could we not ask the whole group "Who got more than five" as everyone can then shout "Me". If we single out a player and they shout "Two" and other players shout "Seven or eight " would they think they had failed and be seen by their peers to have failed?

Think about the way you interact with your players and try to avoid any conflict or tension. Promote and encourage your players.

What can we do with this drill to make it more competitive?

Can we incorporate 1 vs. 1 play?

Split the group into pairs, the pairs should be matched by ability. Number each partner 1 and 2. The number 1 starts with the ball and in 30 seconds tries to dribble through as many cone gates as possible. During this time the number 2 acts as a referee and counts the number of gates.

After 30 seconds they swap roles and whichever player dribbled through the most gates is the winner.

Can we now use these pairs to increase the difficulty and add pressure to the player on the ball?

How about putting all the pairs back into the square but with the number 1 (dribbler) and the number 2 (defender). So now we play 30 seconds or a minute again with the dribbler trying to go through as many gates as possible but this time the defender is trying to win the ball back off their partner. If the defender wins the ball then they become the dribbler. Which player dribbles through the most gates?

Make sure to play at least twice with both the number 1 and number 2 getting a chance to start with the ball.

Now we have introduced a defender to the drill we should look at the other problems this creates.

Dribbling 4 – Dribbling Moves

Close ball control is only part of the dribbling skills your players will need. All the drills so far have looked at improving close ball control and being comfortable on the ball. This will enable our players to keep hold of the ball against opponents in a game, but how will they dribble past them or take them on?

Lets look at a simple drill where we can ask our players to take on and beat a defender. In this drill we will use a 10x20 yard coned channel with a defender standing halfway along. The attackers line up at each end of the channel.

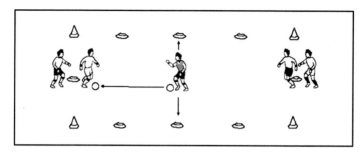

The defender starts with the ball, as they always need to be prepared. The defender then passes the ball to the first attacker who dribbles forward and attempts to take them on. The object of the drill is for the attacker to get past the defender and reach the other end of the channel with the ball still under control. The attacker must remain within the channel and the defender can only move sideways as shown. When the player completes their attempt they join the back of the other queue. The drill repeats but this time the defender passes the ball to the attacker at the front of the opposite queue. Remember to switch the defender regularly so everyone gets the chance to take on a player.

What are we going to coach?

Firstly ignore the defender. This is a dribbling drill and so we should concentrate solely on coaching the attacker and how they can dribble past the defender. In all the previous drills we have looked at close ball control, using both feet, lots of small touches and keeping the head up. In this drill we will take all those key points and add disguise or a "move".

A dribbling "move" is a movement, which throws the defender off balance so the attacker can get round them. A "move" could be an attacker dropping their right shoulder to appear to be moving right only to actually go left. The photographs below show an attacker dropping their right shoulder to appear to the defender to be going right. This is to off balance the defender and disguises the fact that they actually intend to go left.

*Coaching*the*Coach*

Look at the picture sequence and make sure you can perform the "move" yourself, as you will need to demonstrate to the players.

Lets breakdown the whole movement logically, what will you coach first?

The first coaching point is for the player to have a positive attitude believing they will beat the defender. They should not be intimidated by the challenge but relish it. Promote this belief in your players and encourage them to try different ways to get around the players. Keep the session upbeat and applaud player's new ideas and tricks.

The next thing we should coach is the decision. Which "move" are they going to use to get round the defender? They should decide early and stick to the decision. Any indecision will result in failure. If the attempt to beat the defender fails ask your player why? Was it because they were indecisive and had not made up their mind? Was it because they changed their mind at the last minute? Explain that the timing of the player's decision is critical, too late and they will run into the defender.

The third logical coaching point is the "move" or disguise itself. The whole secret to a "move" being successful is the disguise. How much effort your players put into trying to persuade the defender to believe they are going in a direction is paramount. This is the key to moving the defender in this direction and leaving them wrong footed so the attacker can go the other way.

What is there left to coach?

Exploit the space. The player should always accelerate away into the space created by moving the defender. Why? So the defender cannot get back and make a recovery tackle.

Can you improve this "move"?

If the defender is watching the ball then an upper body movement is not going to be seen by the defender. This means the disguise will not fool them. We need to think about the legs of the dribbling player. Ask your players if they watch matches on the television. Do they play football video games? Have they seen a move performed by a player on television or in a video game? What did they do? Can they demonstrate to the other players or explain it?

Ask them all to watch out for new tricks and see if they can explain them or even coach their team-mates to do them.

We will look at the "Scissors" sometimes known as a "Step Over" movement.

We use the same four key coaching points, what were they?

1. Positive attitude
2. Decision
3. Technique of the "move"
4. Exploit the Space

The only difference from just dropping the shoulder is the addition of the movement of the feet. This is to double the disguise. Both the dropping of the shoulder and the movement of the feet need to coincide to double the impact of the disguise.

So for the "Scissors" move we need a positive attitude. The player needs to be absolutely positive they will get past the defender. The Decision to use the scissors to get past the defender needs to be taken early. This leads to a controlled and thoughtful approach to the defender. Now we move onto the disguise or the "Scissors" movement.

Look at the picture sequence above and make sure you can perform the "Move" yourself, as you will need to demonstrate to the players.

We will break down the technique of the move now into two phases the disguise and the contact. Contact meaning the contact of foot on ball.

The disguise is a sweep around the front of the ball with the foot hovering very close to the grass. The foot should move from the inside of the ball out, brushing past the inside of the ball with the outside of the foot. If we imagine the ball to be a clock face, the right foot starts at the 5:00 O'clock position and moves clockwise around the ball setting down at 2:00 O'clock. At the same time the player should dip their right shoulder to look as if they are about to sprint off to the right. This is the disguise, which we need to use to off balance the defender and make them take that step to the right

CoachingtheCoach

The left foot can then be brought forward, the outside of the left foot kicking through the centre of the ball at the 5 O'clock position. This will push the ball 45 degrees to the left along the ground and into the space created by moving the defender to the right.

We should now encourage our players to sprint into the space after performing their "Scissors" move?

How can we progress and increase the challenge?

The defender is currently limited and can only move sideways. The drill can progress with the defender being able to move anywhere. The defender could pass to the attacker and then close them down by following the pass. This will mean the attacker needs to make a decision even quicker. The defender can also chase after the attacker should they get round them. This will promote the attacker sprinting away from the defender.

Would we have to practise this "move" in a drill with a defender?

No, our players could practise the "scissors" whilst dribbling about in our original 20x20 dribbling drill. For younger players the coaching points could be taught within this environment before the challenge of a defender is introduced. This will get your players used to the technique of the "scissors" move and allow for repetitive practice.

What have we missed out?

We have not tried the scissors going in the other direction.

We need to change the disguise. The left shoulder should be dropped and the left foot swept around the ball. We now pretend to sprint left disguising the intended movement to the right, taking the ball away with the outside of the right foot.

This is a simple dribbling "move" which is used by many players in many games. If perfected it can be a very productive way of taking on and beating a defender.

Challenge your players and ask them if they have seen or invented other ways of beating the defender. Can they show their team-mates?

Dribbling 5 – Confined Space Dribbling

Let us now look at our final dribbling drill, which we might use for our better or older players. We will challenge them to dribble the ball about within a very tight confined area. We will also add other players to further challenge their control and dribbling skills.

We can go back to almost our original drill. This time instead of a 20 × 20 yard coaching square we will use the very confined space of a 4 × 4 yard square.

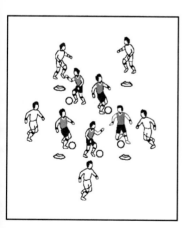

We will show this drill with 10 players, but you can change the size of the confined space dependant on the number of players you get. Put five players in the square with a ball each. The other five can spread around the outside of the coned square.

We will work the players inside the square for approximately 30 seconds and then we can switch them over.

The players around the outside can watch and learn while performing static stretches or generally keeping on their toes and alert.

This drill is simple, players dribble about with their ball within the square for 30 seconds. They should not lose control of the ball or come out of the square. This drill is teaching our players close control and dribbling skills due to the tight playing area and other players around them.

Can we develop again from the drill coaching the players? How can we influence the players? What can we do to improve the challenge?

How can we coach and improve the players?

We need to highlight the use of both feet and lots of small touches. Players will have to use the inside, outside and sole of the foot to keep the ball under close control. They have to keep their heads up and eyes open to see the players and space around them.

We should push our players, always asking them to try and play at a faster tempo. We can encourage them to try a scissors or a turn to keep changing direction. We can ask our players to challenge themselves. Can they go faster, can they include a scissors with their weaker foot?

Can we see how hard they can push themselves for 30 seconds, putting everything into those short bursts of work? If they are going to fail or make a mistake, either coming out of the square or losing control of the ball. Then they should fail trying to go faster or trying something new. This is a training session where we practice to improve. If our players stay within their comfort zone and never push themselves onto try new things they will never improve. We need to provide an environment where failure is accepted as something that needs to be overcome on the path to success.

If we always do what we always did, then we will always get what we always got. Encourage your players to experiment, try new things, and go faster.

Every 30 seconds or so swap the players in the middle with the players on the outside. Each set of players can have a couple of goes each in the middle of the square.

How else can we progress this drill?

1.   We can reduce the square to 3 x 3 yards.
2.   We can add passing and receiving skills into the drill.
3.   Incorporate one-two passes with the players on the outside.
4.   The players have to pass to different players on different sides of the square.

What can you coach?

This drill can be used to progress onto all kinds of coaching points. We will discuss two and hopefully it will make you think about coaching and what we can say and do to affect and improve our players.

The players on the outside need to call the player with the ball to tell them they are free to receive the ball. The players on the edge should call the players name. If the dribbling players just pass out to any free player then that player could receive two or three balls at a time. Players need to communicate verbally or make eye contact and be ready at all times to receive or pass the ball. See the diagram left.

The player receiving the ball inside the square also needs to find space. Players will pass the ball out to a player on the edge then stay still and receive it back in the middle of the square amongst all the other players. We can introduce passing and moving to the edge of the square, almost next to the player they have passed to. They can then turn to face the centre of the square and receive the ball on the "half turn". This will give them time and space moving everyone from the congestion in the middle to see the whole playing area and where they can go next.

*Coaching*the*Coach*

This drill can be used for all skill levels you just need to vary the organisation. A larger area with fewer players can be used for the younger or newer players. Small tight areas with more players involved should be used to challenge the better or older players.

In all cases the coaching points are the same. It will be more about the amount you coach and the level of detail you go into. With more experienced players you can progress the drill quickly and pick up on any mistake rather than concentrate on getting just one coaching point correct.

Before you coach your next dribbling drill think about what you want to try and do to improve your players. Consider their skill levels and how quickly they learn and improve.

This chapter has taken us from simply supervising our players dribbling around in a square using their favourite foot, to a pressured dribbling drill. We have also introduced defenders. We have demonstrated the virtues of speed. We have looked at using both feet and all the parts of the foot (the instep, outside and sole). We have also looked at ways of keeping the player's head up to check what's around them.

As a coach we have also moved from simply using a standard drill to thinking about changing it to accommodate a different number of players or coaches. We have also started to analyse our player's skill levels and adapting the drills to suit their needs.

We are now beginning the transition from supervisor to coach.

*Coaching*the*Coach -*
Running with the Ball

Running with the Ball

Running With the Ball 1 – Speed

What is the difference between dribbling and running with the ball?

Dribbling is not done at any great speed and the ball is always under close control. It is used in a confined space or with opponents nearby. Running with the ball is done to capitalise quickly on a space on the pitch in front of the player. The player kicks the ball into the space and sprints after it. The ball is kicked ahead to enable the player to sprint at full speed.

The first drill we will look at promotes speed. The drill is a simple 5x20 yard channel. You will need to change the size dependant on the age and skill of your players. In this drill the player simply sprints with the ball along the channel from one end to the other.

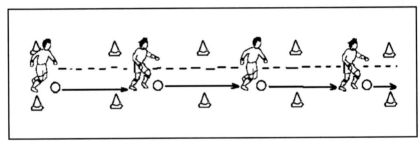

Why is it a very tight channel?

We need to promote the player running in a straight line. The ball needs to be played directly in front of them. This is because the quickest way between two points is a straight line.

In this drill we can concentrate on coaching the contact between the kicking foot and ball. The contact should be with the laces of the nearest foot through the middle of the ball.

What do we mean by the nearest foot, and why is it important?

The nearest foot means the foot that naturally reaches the ball whilst sprinting. If the player breaks their stride pattern to enable them to kick the ball with their favourite foot then speed will be lost. So as the player sprints the foot nearest the ball should be used to kick the ball and therefore keep up the speed of the run. The ball should be kicked roughly 7 yards ahead of the player before being kicked again. Older players may take a touch every 10 yards and you will probably want to lengthen the drill channel.

The coach should emphasise the requirement for speed. This means the run should be direct and straight, with the least amount of touches to cover the distance.

How could you challenge your players to go faster?

If you timed them through the channel then they would get an idea of their own speed. Coach them to be direct and take fewer touches without breaking their stride pattern and see if their times improve.

Running With the Ball 2 – Two Runners

Now we will progress to look at the other coaching points that go into running with the ball rather than just the technique. This drill involves a coned rectangle, cones in each corner only. The rectangle is 20x30 yards. The players are split and half of the players stand at one corner of the rectangle and the others stand at the corner diagonally opposite.

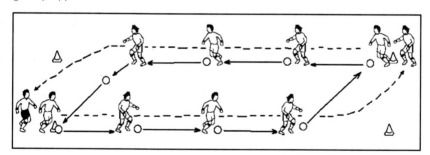

The first player in each queue has a ball and on the coaches command sprints directly forward running with the ball. The players have to sprint straight at the cone ahead of them and not toward the line of players opposite.

When they get within 5 yards of the end cone they pass the ball diagonally across to the first player in the other line. That player can then sprint forward with the ball and repeat the drill.

What will we coach?

The player's attitude is the first thing to coach. Our players need a positive attitude and first touch. This is to get the ball out of the player's feet. The player should let the ball come across their body and kick it forward using the instep of the back foot.

For example the player in the top right of the diagram will take the first touch with the instep of their right foot. The ball is passed from the bottom player up and across the front of their body. This allows them to play forward with instep of the right, or back foot. The ball will now be kicked straight forward giving the player a straight and fast run between the two points.

The second coaching point is for the player to have their head up in between touches. In a game environment the player needs to see the situation on the field and options around them. All the time the player is running the game environment is changing. Defenders are recovering and attackers are sprinting forward. They need to see what is happening and be aware. If they do not get their head up they might not see the defender approaching to cut off the run. This means during this drill we need to coach our players to keep their head up in between touches.

The final coaching point is the end product. This is the final pass taken after the run. The end pass should be played into the space directly in front of the player at the front of the other queue. It should also be played at a suitable pace for them to be positive and attack the ball at speed.

Can you remember the coaching points?

1. Attitude - The player needs a positive attitude and first touch.
2. Head Up - The player should have their head up in between touches.
3. Contact - The laces of the nearest boot should contact through the centre of the ball.
4. End product – The final pass needs to be played in front of the next player.

Running with the ball seems such an easy task but if you coach your players through these critical stages they will improve. They will be more aware of what is around them during a game and more importantly they will be quicker.

*Coaching*the***Coach*** - Passing

Passing

Passing 1 – Passing Gates

We can start with the same "Through the Gates" drill, page 13 so lets remember the organisation.

What did we say about our cones and the colours?

We have our original 20 x 20 grid marked out with white cones but with a series of blue gates or goals placed within the square. The gates are two cones placed roughly one or two feet apart. Make sure we have five or six more gates than players. Split the group into pairs, the pairs should be matched by ability. Number each partner 1 and 2 and give number 2 the ball to start with. The idea is simply to pass the ball through the gate to your partner without hitting the gate (cones).

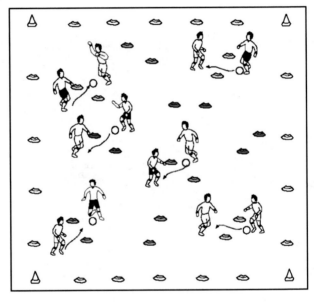

As a coach what might you expect to see from younger or inexperienced players?

The favourite foot syndrome is back again and possibly you will see players not trapping the ball first and just swinging their foot at the ball as it rolls towards them. Passes are too hard or too soft; players toe poking the ball and wayward passes could also be seen.

As the coach what will you do, let the players carry on and eventually learn from the drill or start to coach?

What will you coach first?

We need to introduce trapping the ball so that the ball is stationary prior to their pass, that way we can work on the pass and the contact of their foot on the ball.

It is difficult for very young players to judge the speed of the ball. So controlling the ball by putting their foot on it can be difficult, even though it is the method they very often try to adopt.

Younger players should trap the ball by using their instep (largest area of the foot) and cushioning the ball. Once they have the ball still in front of them and only then can we begin to practise the pass.

This simple drill now gives us the opportunity to actually coach a series of movements, which will lead to a good pass.

Firstly we are looking for an accurate pass over a short distance so would the instep (side foot) pass be the best choice?

The instep is the largest area of the foot and therefore easier to contact with the centre of the ball resulting in a straight controlled pass.

Now to break down the movements, the standing foot should be next to the ball, but why? If the standing foot is either in front of or back from the ball then it is very difficult to cleanly make contact with the centre of the ball. Contact with the ball too high will bounce it into the ground or scuff the ball resulting in loss of power and accuracy. Contact with the base of the ball will see it rise or be chipped up again with loss of accuracy.

With the standing foot next to the ball it enables an easy contact through the centre of the ball allowing a straight pass along the ground. The toes of the standing foot should also point to the target, in this case their partner through the goal.

Remember the contact point between foot and ball is paramount to accuracy. So if you see a scuffed or topped pass you need to correct it. Coach your players by demonstrating how moving their standing foot next to the ball will make the pass easier and more accurate. As the coach you have to spot the problem and solve it.

What other point's can you think of that will lead to a good pass?

The speed or weight of the pass:- too hard and their partner will be unable to control it, too soft and it will not reach them.

What should we look for when we try to coach players about the weight of the pass?

Any increase in speed of the kicking foot or follow through will directly increase the weight or speed of the pass.

If you see a problem what are you going to do?

Stop the player and gently explain why you have stopped them. Demonstrate and show them why they made the mistake and how they can correct it.

Have they learnt; how do you know?

Get the player to try the pass again incorporating your advice, was it correct or did they repeat the problem? If it was correct they have learnt and progressed, if not demonstrate again and explain until they understand.

Does trapping the ball prior to making a controlled instep / side foot pass make any difference? What do you see comparing the performance originally to how the players perform now? What do the players think, why not ask them?

Can we create some fun?

We could introduce competition by working in pairs how many goals (passes through the gate) can they score in 30 seconds?

How well did the pairs perform and did the extra challenge make a difference, have they stopped trapping the ball and how about the weight of the pass. More importantly did you spot it?

Could we use this drill for more advanced players, how would you alter the drill?

1.   Smaller goals.
2.   The players could stand further apart.
3.   They could trap right foot, pass left foot then alternate trap left foot,
        pass right foot and so on.
4.   How about moving onto one touch alternate foot passing.
5.   Increase the speed of the passes, how many in 10 seconds.

How can we progress the drill further, can we add some movement?

Lets go back to the dribbling drill and incorporate it. The players are already in pairs so lets start them at their current goal or "start position" make sure they know this is their "start position" and as such the starting point for the drill. This will enable us to begin the drill from this same controlled start point each time.

In this drill the players work in pairs; player 1 starts with the ball and passes it to player 2 through their "starting position" goal. Player 2 can then dribble the ball around the grid to find any other free goal, which they can pass through to return the ball to player 1. This is repeated over a set time.

How many passes through different gates or goals did each team score?

Have a think about this drill and how many things you can coach.

Remember during this drill we should concentrate on all the points we have discussed to create a good pass. We could also touch on the basic points of dribbling like keeping the head up to look for the next goal and their partner. Also communication can help with partners shouting or pointing to a free goal.

Passing 2 – Passing 3 v 1

Let's progress to another favourite drill we see time and time again on training pitches around the world. In a 10-yard square we see 3 attackers on the edge and a single defender in the centre of the square. The drill begins with the three attackers trying to pass to each other around the square without letting the defender intercept a pass and get the ball.

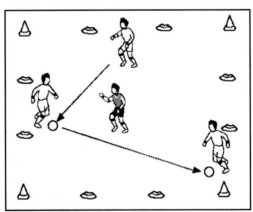

For very young players you may want to make it easier - How can you do that?

Start with all four players passing to each other within the square with no defender and therefore no pressure.

However you start this drill, with or without a defender it can still be used to assess the pass of the players. We look at the weight of the pass, too soft and the ball will not reach its intended destination, too hard and the receiving player will not control the ball.

The accuracy of the pass can also be coached, as the pass has to go directly to one of the attackers teammates and obviously not the defender if he is introduced.

What coaching points affect the quality of the pass?

1.   Approach - slightly from the side to give enough room to make a comfortable pass. If the player moves straight onto the ball then there is a possibility to toe poke the ball.
2.   Body shape - the non-kicking foot should be next to the ball with the toe pointing in the direction of the intended pass. The head should be steady and the arms out to balance the player.
3.   Contact - through the centre of the ball.
4.   Follow through - this helps the guidance of the pass its accuracy and the power, more follow through results in more power.

This drill with the introduction of the defender will also teach players the value of space. They will have to move along the line to get into a position where they can receive the ball.

What might you see in your players and coach when we look at creating space?

If a player stands directly behind a defender they will never receive the ball because the player with the ball cannot pass through the defender. Stop the drill show the player that they cannot receive the ball and demonstrate where they would be better to stand, in space.

Who else might get in the way of a pass?

Another attacker could move into a position between the player with the ball and a second attacker. If we take a look again at the picture above but this time imagine that the defender, in the middle of the photograph is another attacker. This player we can imagine has moved in close for a short pass. The second attacker, further away, is now blocked off and cannot receive a pass. The furthest player will again have to be the player to make a movement into space. The furthest player is always the player to move as they can see the path of the pass and all the players in front of them. The nearer player cannot see any players behind them easily.

Can you spot the mistakes and correct them; can you demonstrate and explain to them a correctly played pass?

Was the pass accurate? Was it the correct weight, did it reach the player or was it so hard and fast that they could not control it? Were the other players in space, ready and able to receive a pass?

What might you try to introduce or coach to the better or older players?

Some ideas include disguising the pass, pretend to play a pass, stop, turn, and play it in a different direction and or with the other foot.

Can they use the outside of their foot to flick it in the opposite direction to the standard instep pass? Demonstrate all these points individually and coach or educate your players.

Remember all the points we looked for in a good pass, are your players competent? Can you see anything being done incorrectly? Can you make the difference? Can you coach them?

How can we challenge them further, Can we introduce some goals?

We will give a "Goal" to the attackers for every 6 consecutive passes made and a "Goal" to the defender for every two interceptions or tackles when they win the ball.

What is happening to the drill?

Has the introduction of the challenge and the goals been successful or are the players suffering under the pressure. Have they reverted to blind passes and quick kicks just to get rid of the responsibility of having the ball and needing to make a good pass?

If so what will you do to take back control?

Calm down the drill and set out the rules for a successful pass and demonstrate, let them play again, is it back under control?

As the coach we need to assess the success of the drill and change the rules as and when required. Is introducing six consecutive passes working or is it too many or too few? Is it completely beyond them, should we just award "Goals" with successful passes?

For better players you may feel it is too easy to achieve six passes, apart from increasing the number of passes required to gain a "Goal" what else might you introduce?

How about letting all the players move anywhere within the square or introducing 4 vs. 2 in a larger 20 x 20 yard square.

Assess how the players cope. Make the drill incrementally more or less difficult as required.

When preparing your coaching session you should have a good idea of what your players can and can't do. Always prepare the session and drills with their skill levels in mind and most importantly what you want to coach and improve.

What is the problem of using the instep to pass a ball?

The defender can easily read where the pass is going by watching the passing players leg being pulled back. They will see the movement of the player's leg and the line in which the foot moves and therefore where the player wants to kick the ball.

How can you coach or explain?

We can demonstrate the instep kicking action, pulling our leg back in line with where we want to pass the ball and stop the foot directly before contact with the ball. Ask the players if they can tell where we wanted to pass the ball?

How about lining up three cones red, blue and yellow all ten yards apart. Would the players be able to shout out which cone we where aiming at if we stood ten yards away and lined up an instep pass? Yes.

So what do you do, this is an advantage for the defender?

CoachingtheCoach

Using the same three coloured cones in a line and standing in front of them with the ball at your feet. Line up a pass with the laces of your boot, a driven pass. Stop the kicking action again just before impact. Where is the pass going? Straight?

A driven pass off the laces can be flicked directly ahead or two either side at the last moment. Demonstrate the three passes going to the three different cones. Flick the ball off the middle laces of the boot then just to the right and then just to the left flicking the ball toward all the cones in turn.

Disguise!

This is disguising the pass, now the defender is unsure of where the pass is going.

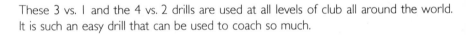

These 3 vs. I and the 4 vs. 2 drills are used at all levels of club all around the world. It is such an easy drill that can be used to coach so much.

We can demonstrate and coach all the points of a good pass leading to an accurate and correctly weighted pass. Here are the coaching points again can you elaborate on the trigger words?

1. Approach
2. Body shape
3. Contact
4. Follow Through

What else can we use this drill to coach?

We can also look at disguising the pass, turning with the ball or even dribbling past a player or shielding the ball in a tight area. Another coaching point and probably the most important role is that of the player without the ball. Creating space to receive it. This involves the receiving player moving into a position where the player with the ball has an opportunity to pass to them. Do not allow the defender or another attacker to stand directly between the player with the ball and the receiver as this will block a pass.

Passing 3 – 4 v 2

Now we will take the 4 vs. 2 drill and tweak it to increase the momentum and challenge. We will use the 20x20 yard coned grid but this time split the players into three equal teams. In our diagram below we have six players split into three teams of two. The teams wear White, Black and Grey bibs.

The concept of the drill is for two of the teams to work together as a team of four against a single team of two defenders. The diagram shows the Grey and Black teams playing together against the two White defenders. The drill now follows the rules of a normal 4 Vs 2 passing drill. The four players work together to try and keep the ball away from the two defenders.

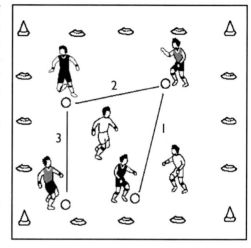

The twist on the normal 4 vs. 2 drill happens when the defending pair wins possession of the ball.

If a player in the attacking team loses possession of the ball then that player's team becomes the defending team. For example, the Black team become defenders if the white defender intercepts the first pass shown. In this case the White and Grey teams would now join forces as the attacking four against the Black defenders. The attackers now have a forfeit should they lose possession of the ball. They are deemed to have lost the ball in the following circumstances.

1.   They can have a pass intercepted.
2.   They can misplace a pass, which goes out of the square or
      to a defender
3.   The defender can tackle them.
4.   They can run the ball out of the square.

In all these cases the defending team win the ball and the player who made the error commits their team to the forfeit of defending. The successful defending team join forces with the remaining attacking pair to form a new attacking team.

We have now increased the challenge and naturally the work rate of our players. The defenders don't want to stay defenders. We have created a very realistic challenge for our attackers. They will need to see the correct pass and play it perfectly as the defenders will want to seize upon any error.

What will you coach?

In this drill we have moved from coaching key points and techniques to watching our players and looking for mistakes. In this drill we want our players to think and play at a high tempo so we need to let them play.

We should stop the drill when the mistake is made. What did they do wrong? Did they wait too long before passing the ball? Was there a player positioned to receive the pass? Did they need to turn or disguise a pass? Was the technique of the pass wrong, too hard, too soft, or not accurate? Did the defender close them down and if not, did they even need to pass the ball?

All these points could be reasons as to why possession was lost. They are all points, which you need to be able to see during the drill or game and explain to your players. This is not something that you will be able to do tomorrow. As you coach, watch and experience the mistakes you will learn. Coaching is not just knowing what to coach it is seeing the problem and knowing how to correct it.

Passing 4 – Passing Team Challenge

Now we will continue our progression and look at a drill, which can be used by the better or older players. In this drill we use two squares one grey-coned square inside the larger white-coned square. The central grey square size depends on the amount of players and also their skill level.

In our diagram we have fourteen players. We will be using a 10x10 foot grey square inside a much larger 30x30 white square. The diagram below shows the organisation and the way the two teams start out.

In the central grey square we have five (grey bibs) Vs two (white bibs). The drill is very similar to the 3 vs. I and 4 vs. 2 drills. The five grey players try to keep the ball by passing it amongst themselves while the two white "defenders" try to challenge and intercept to win the ball. Play is restricted to within the central 10x10 square and the rest of the white team; those outside the central square are initially not involved.

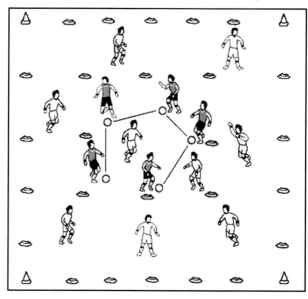

If the two players win the ball or the ball comes out of the 10x10 square then all players become active and play reverts to the 30x30 square. The white team now plays keep ball with their nine players Vs the five grey-bibbed players. All the players can now move anywhere within the 30x30 square. This means any white can move through the 10x10 square and any grey can move anywhere in the 30x30 to win back possession of the ball.

Play stops only when the grey bibbed team win back the ball. The drill then restarts as

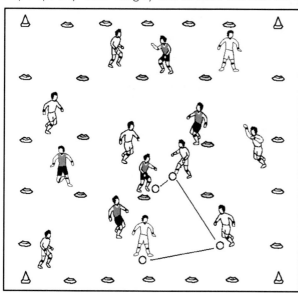

before with the five greys vs. the two whites within the 10x10 square. The seven white players in the larger square are again initially not involved.

This drill requires the grey players to keep possession within a very tight playing area, the 10x10 square. The drill then focuses on the white team spreading out and keeping possession in a larger area.

What can we use the drill to coach?

We can coach the different techniques of passing over both short and long distances. We can look at the lofted pass to enable us to get the ball from one side of the large square over the defenders to the free space on the other. We can look at creating space, receiving the ball on the half turn. We can coach receiving the ball with a defender very close and shielding the ball. This will also allow us to coach support play from their other teammates.

The drill will also add pressure on the player with the ball who has to make the pass, especially in the smaller central square. The drill can be used to coach the players when and where they should pass the ball. We can also progress to coach dribbling and turns.

Spot the mistake then explain clearly and correct it. Demonstrate how it should be done correctly and the difference it makes. Please think about this drill, try it a couple of times and see what you can do.

Remember the skill levels of your players and the theme of your coaching session. For adults you may want to remind them of many coaching points to improve and stimulate them. For younger players be brief and concise and stick to the theme of your session.

*Coaching*the***Coach* - Defending**

Defending

Defending I – Defending I v I

For this drill we will go back to our original 20x20 grid and split the group into pairs. The pairs should be split by ability so both partners are equally matched. One player is the attacker and one is the defender. The idea is simply that the attacker tries to keep the ball while the defender tries to win the ball to become the attacker and reverse the roles. Neither the attacker nor their ball is allowed outside the grid. If they do stray outside the grid then the defender wins possession and the drill continues with the roles reversed.

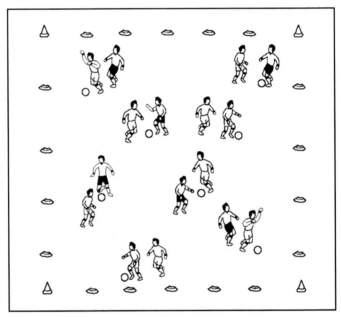

How close does the defender need to be to the attacker?

The defender should be two or three feet from the attacker this gives them a clear unobstructed view of the ball. If the defender was closer the attacker's body or legs might mask the defenders sight of the ball.

If the defender cannot see the ball then they may react to any movement, body swerve or step over trick the attacker may adopt. Due to this the defender must see and concentrate on the position of the ball at all times.

Two to three feet is also a distance from which the defender can reach any loose ball or instigate a tackle. They can also feint a tackle putting the pressure back onto the attacker and trying to force them into a mistake. By feinting to tackle the defender can make the attacker think more about keeping hold of the ball rather than attacking and trying to beat them.

Demonstrate this to the players. If you act as the attacker shielding the ball, ask a player to stand in a position where they can see the ball. Ask your players if they are also close enough to affect the attacker by pretending or being able to make a tackle? Demonstrate the distance and what effect it can have.

What else can we coach?

The body shape of the defender is critical. They should be half turned and not square on to the attacker. Why? A square facing defender is not in a position to turn quickly should the ball be played past them. If the defender is half turned, balanced with knees slightly bent they are always in a position to quickly turn off either foot. A half turned defender also natural pushes an attacker in one direction. Ask your players which way and how? A defender half turned with their right foot forward will naturally face about 45 degrees left which opens the left side of the pitch to the attacker. While a defender with their left foot forward will face right, which opens the right side. See the diagrams below, Right foot forward below left and left foot forward below right.

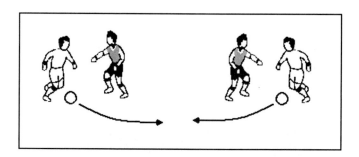

Why would this stance be good for a defender?

The defender can use this half turned stance to try and push the attacker into a tight corner or out against a sideline. Alternatively the defender may show them inside into two other defenders giving them a numerical advantage against the attacker. Demonstrate this half turned 45-degree defending position to your players. Can they see the effect it has shutting off one side to the attacker.

What else do we need to tell our players?

When should they make the tackle or challenge for the ball? Firstly defenders need to be patient. Once the defender is in a good position, watching the ball, they can wait for an opportunity to win the ball. If the defender is impatient they may dive in at the wrong time and leave the attacker with an easy job of beating them. By being patient, watching the ball and being in the defending position the emphasis is back with the attacker.

It is now the attacker who has the problem of how to beat the defender. This will lead to the attacker trying a trick or dummy to off balance the defender and beat them. If the defender stays focused on the ball the time will come when the attacker is off balance or the ball is out of their control. This could be when they attempt to run past the defender, turn or try to dummy. At this time their body weight is all on one foot and the ball will be available for the defender to win cleanly.

Which foot should they tackle with?

The tackle needs to be made with the nearest foot, as this will be the quickest tackle. The defender does not have time to manoeuvre into a position to make the tackle with a favourite foot. Demonstrate that the tackle needs to be swift and with the nearest foot otherwise the opportunity to tackle will be lost.

What is the last resort?

A sliding tackle or any tackle where the defender goes to ground is the last resort. A defender should stay on their feet as long as possible. As soon as they go to ground they are out of the game. A defender making a sliding tackle must be certain they will get the ball. Make your players aware that they should adopt a good defending position and hold up the attacker.

Defending 2 – Defending 3 v 1

Let us have a think about what other kind of drills we can use to coach defending. Any passing drill or dribbling drill that contains a defender can be turned into a defending drill. Just remember to only coach the one topic, defending. So if we use the passing drill 3 v 1 we ignore the passing and the attackers and concentrate on what the defender is and should be doing.

The drill is a 10x10 yard square with 3 attackers on the edge and a single defender in the centre of the square. The drill begins with the three attackers trying to pass to each other around the square. The defender tries to intercept a pass or tackle a player and win the ball.

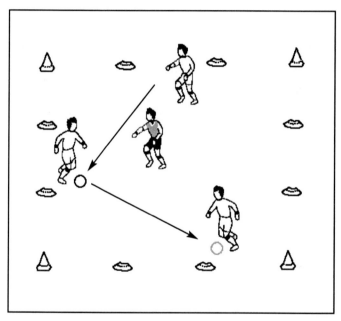

We have the same coaching points from the last drill to expand upon again. These are the distance of the defender from the attacker. The need to always watch the ball and be in a position to be able to affect the attacker and win the ball. The defenders body shape and the half turned defending position. The defender needs patience to wait and time the tackle. Tackle swiftly at the given opportunity with the nearest foot. Do not dive in and definitely do not go to ground unless certain of winning the ball.

There are more attackers and therefore passing in this drill so what else can we coach?

The first thing we need to look at is the defenders movement. The defender should move as the ball is kicked. Why? While the ball is at the attacker's feet they should be poised on the half turn patiently waiting to make the tackle or turn and sprint. As the ball is played they need to get into a new position as quickly as possible.

The defender needs to be watching the ball as it is played they should move as quickly as possible either to win the ball or close down the player receiving the ball. If they can intercept the ball then that is the first priority. If they cannot intercept they must get to the receiving player as fast as possible and adopt a good defending position.

What affects these two outcomes?

Ask your players what they think. The defender needs to focus on the weight and accuracy of the pass and make a decision. The decision is the second point that we need to coach our defenders. If the pass is weak or inaccurate then they need to make an early decision and sprint to intercept it. If the ball is accurate and strong enough to reach the other player then they should sprint to a good defensive position.

Can you demonstrate the two scenarios of a good and bad pass? Show the defenders the two different movements either to intercept or adopt a new position.

How can being half turned affect the attackers?

By getting half turned and standing in a position, which prevents the ball going to one of the attackers, the defender reduces the options for the attacker with the ball. It also means the defender is pushing the attacker into making the open pass. The one they are aware of and can react to easily and quickest. See the diagram below where the defender has cut off the pass to the player at the top of the grid. The defender is also right foot forward. This opens their body to any pass to the player at the bottom of the grid. They are in a great position to close down the player with the ball.

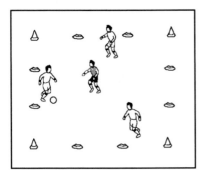

When the pass is made to the attacker at the bottom the defender can sprint toward them and try to get to the ball first.

Remember to only coach one theme especially with younger players. If you begin coaching defending don't switch to passing, then a bit of dribbling and back to defending. The players will only get confused if you jump from theme to theme.

*Coaching*the*Coach -*
Turns

Turns

Turns 1 – Simple Turns

Returning to our original drill, which involves our squad of players in a 20 x 20 coned square. All the players have a ball and begin dribbling around within the square. The drill provides a natural challenge as other players are in the same space so everyone has to keep their heads and eyes up. This is to see all the players around them and the coaching square so they can turn away from others or the edge of the square.

We will use this simple square as our coaching area. We can make everyone within it hear and see us. Especially if we move into the centre and demonstrate the turn we want to coach them.

So what do we want to do?

As a coach we now want to educate our players with a few simple turns. These will be used at any standard of football they aspire to play from now until the day they hang up their boots.

For every turn there are a few basic key points the players must adhere to. As the coach we need to concentrate on these before we move onto the technique of the turn itself.

For all turns to be performed well what must we make sure our players do? Think about how a turn is performed and the stages leading up to, during and after the turn.

Every turn can be broken down into 5 key stages. Can you think what they are?

1. Approach - The approach should be controlled moving forward with the ball.
2. Protection - The player should use their legs and body to protect the ball. Always turn away from the defender and never into them.
3. Body Shape - The player should be well balanced, knees bent and arms out for balance with the head steady.
4. Contact – The contact on the ball and the technique of the particular turn, which we will go through as we look at each of the turns
5. Exploit the space - After executing a turn the player should accelerate away leaving any defender unable to recover.

How did you do?

Now we can concentrate on each particular stage which when put together creates a great turn.

If a player makes a mistake on any of these stages then the coach can quietly question them. Would it be a good idea to stop everyone and highlight a player and the mistake in front of the whole group? No. Bring the player to the side while everyone else continues to practice. Demonstrate the problem and solution and watch the player perform to see if they have understood.

Each of the key stages can be coached and demonstrated to the whole group. Isolating a particular player and mistake will not breed confidence or create an environment conducive to trying new skills. Why? Because the players will be scared to fail and be embarrassed at their mistakes in front of others.

Lets get all our players moving about again with a ball each within the coaching square. We can start with coaching the "Inside Hook"

Firstly it's up to the coach to stop the group and make sure they are all watching and listening,

"STOP STAND STILL"

A precise and loud shout to get the players attention, which means they all stand silent with the ball at their feet waiting for you to coach!

With smaller players you may want them to also put the sole of the right foot on the top of the ball and a hand in the air. This way you know the ball is still and they are ready, waiting and listening.

Inside Hook

Look at the picture sequence below and make sure you can perform the turn yourself, as you will need to demonstrate it to the players.

Note the player reaches beyond the ball with their closest leg. The player then uses the instep of their furthest foot spinning round to contact the middle of the far side of the ball making it come directly backwards, the player can then sprint off back in the direction they came.

The coach should demonstrate the turn in the middle of the group so all the players can see and hear clearly.

How will you know they have understood your demonstration and explanation?

Watch them try it for themselves.

As the coach walks around the edge of the coaching square they can clearly see all the players within the square performing the turn being coached. It is the perfect coaching position.

If you spot a player that has a problem simply go up to them and quietly explain the problem. Demonstrate the correct turn and let them try it again. Watch and check.

Would it be a good idea for a coach to wander through the centre of the coaching square?

No, You will only get in the way and keeping to the outside you can better observe all your players within.

What will you tell the better players?

How about more disguise to fool an imaginary defender, pretend to sprint forward before turning, take a swing at the ball as if to kick it then turn back.

When you turn which side should the defender be? The side you turn away from or the side you turn into?

The defender should be on the side you turn away from. The opposite side to the side the player turns. This means the body of the player is always between the ball and the defender, shielding the ball.

"STOP STAND STILL"

Outside Hook

Look at the pictures below and make sure you can demonstrate it to the players.

This time the player reaches beyond the ball with the foot furthest from the ball and plants it down. They can then take the ball backwards with the outside of their nearest foot. The player uses the outside of their foot contacting through the middle of the front of the ball, which results in the ball coming directly backwards. The player can then sprint off back in the direction they came.

What can we notice about our players, can we see the favourite foot syndrome returning?

Do players always use the same foot to perform the turns and why is this a problem?

If they use the same foot they can only turn round one way and if the defender is that side of them they will turn straight into them. Encourage your players and coach them to always use both feet.

Step Over

Look at the picture sequence below and make sure you can perform the turn yourself, as you will need to demonstrate it to the players.

In this turn the player reaches over and beyond the ball with the nearest foot to the ball and plants it down. The player can then swivel around through 180 degrees and play

the ball away with the inside of the furthest foot. The inside of this foot strikes cleanly through the middle of the ball sending it back from where they came, the player then sprints off after it.

What are we seeing as we watch all these drills?

Is the player performing the turn and then sprinting away after the turn is made to exploit the space?

We should coach our players and encourage them to exploit the space. This is one of the important points we originally stated as key to a great turn.

Why was it so important?

The whole purpose of performing a turn is to move away from a defender. So after a turn the player should accelaerate away from the defender as fast as possible. Why? The player has to make sure the defender cannot recover to make a tackle.

Remember the five key points we listed at the start of this chapter, can you list them now?

As a coach we should continually explain and demonstrate these five points, which make up the whole turn.

1. Approach - The approach should be controlled moving forward with the ball.
2. Protection - The player should use their legs and body to protect the ball. Always turn away from the defender and never into them.
3. Body Shape - The player should be well balanced, knees bent and arms out for balance with the head steady.
4. Contact – The contact on the ball and the technique of the particular turn, which we will go through as we look at each of the turns
5. Exploit the space - After executing a turn the player should accelerate away leaving any defender unable to recover.

"STOP STAND STILL"

Stop Turn

Look at the picture sequence below and make sure you can perform the turn yourself, as you will need to demonstrate it to the players.

In the stop turn the player stops the ball with the sole of their foot and then continues to jump over the ball. When the player lands their stance should be somewhat like a skateboarder with the ball at the outside of the back foot. The player can then use the outside of the back foot to take the ball away straight back in the direction they came.

When should we perform the stop turn?

When the defender is in front of the player. This turn enables the player to get over the ball and in between the ball and the defender, shielding the ball from the defender.

What else might our more advanced players do to protect the ball?

How about putting the arm out which is nearest the defender to block them from getting to the ball.

"STOP STAND STIILL"

Cryuff Turn

Look at the picture sequences below and make sure you can perform the turn yourself, as you will need to demonstrate it to the players. The first sequence shows the turn from the front.

The second sequence shows the same turn from the side.

In the Cryuff turn the player exaggerates the action of crossing or shooting. After they have planted the standing leg instead of following through with the cross they stop the kicking foot immediately ahead of the ball. The instep of the kicking foot then draws the ball backwards behind the standing leg and away. The contact is with the instep of the foot through the centre of the far side of the ball. The ball is then taken away backwards.

Have a think about what type of characteristics you are looking for in your players when they perform this turn?

Approach straight and purposeful followed by a massively exaggerated attempt to cross or shoot. Promote the exaggeration by extending the arms out for balance. The more purposeful and believable the player can make the action of crossing or shooting the better the disguise. This means more chance of committing the defender to going the wrong way. The player then only needs a small knock back in the other direction with the instep to leave the defender wrong footed.

When a player performs any of these turns the contact on the ball at the point of the turn is critical. Too hard and the ball will shoot away from the player. When a turn is performed the ball should be knocked back but always kept within the players control zone, within reach. The defender will be able to step in and steal the ball if the ball is knocked out of reach.

As the coach should we be making sure our players attempt the Cryuff Turn with both feet?

Of course we should remember to coach all these turns using both feet.

"STOP STAND STIILL"

Drag Back

Look at the picture sequence below and make sure you can perform the turn yourself, as you will need to demonstrate it to the players.

This is a simple turn where the player while going one way puts their sole onto the top of the ball stopping it and rolls it back behind them. The player can then turn backwards to take the ball away with the outside of the same foot that dragged the ball back.

Are you observing the players whilst wandering through the coaching square or are you moving around the outside looking in on your squad?

You are on the outside of the square and see a player with a problem, what do you do?

Quietly pull the player to the side, explaining the problem and demonstrate the solution. Did they understand? How do you know? Watch them perform the turn, was it correct?

What about the better players, which foot should they use to drag the ball back with in a game?

From our five key stages we see that a coaching point is the protection of the ball. So the player should always use the foot furthest from the defender. By using the foot nearest the defender they could drag the ball straight back into them.

If this is the case should we be able to do all the turns going both ways and with both feet?

Yes. Then coach the turns so that all of your players are comfortable using both feet.

"STOP STAND STILL"

With smaller players should we run through all the turns during one session?

If we tried to do all six it would become tiring and very hard for them to remember which turn was which and how each one was performed. Maybe a better option is to concentrate on each one individually. First with the right foot then with the left over six different sessions. As players become more advanced and competent then more turns could be undertaken during any one session. Know the skill level of the players you are coaching and plan accordingly.

All these turns have been undertaken within the 20x20 coaching square. They could be incorporated into a training session straight after the warm up when players are fresh, eager and more likely to take in the technical information and remember it.

There are many drills, which incorporate turns, but to coach them, you need to know what points make up a turn. Be able to determine which stage was the reason for the turn failing and then how to correct it.

Turns – I vs. I

Now we have coached all the turns to our players we need to test them and challenge them again especially our older or better players. In this drill we use a simple 10x20 yard coned channel with a player, serving and receiving at each end. Two players are positioned within the channel. One is the attacker and one is the defender. The defender is shown below in the grey bib.

Firstly the server on the left plays the ball into the attacker.

The attacker now needs to shield the ball from the defender. They then need to execute a turn with the ball to get round the defender and pass it out to the opposite player receiving on the right. The drill can then repeat with the player on the right serving the ball into the attacker who tries to turn the defender and pass it back to the player on the left.

Remember to switch the players so they all get a chance to play as the attacker and the defender.

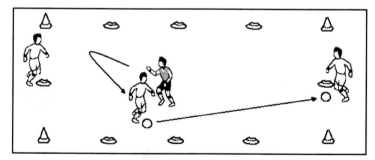

The coaching points are the same for the technique of the turn itself. Can you list them?

1. Approach
2. Protection
3. Body Shape
4. Contact
5. Exploit the space

There is more to this drill than simply executing a technically sound turn. To begin with there is a goal, to get the ball to the player at the other end of the channel. There is also a defender trying to stop them.

What else would we need to consider coaching?

Firstly we need to coach our attacker to create space. They need to move to create an opportunity for the pass. Can the attacker get away from the defender with a late and fast run. If the attacker can get away from the defender it may mean they can receive the ball already half turned. This means there is enough space between the attacker and the defender to enable them to turn and face the defender. Receiving the ball in between them and the defender.

This leads onto the second coaching point, which is to know where the defender is. As the attacker makes a late and fast run they should look over their shoulder to see how near the defender is. If the defender is along way away then the attacker may have time to get half turned. Too near and the attacker cannot get turned and will have to shield the ball. Make sure your attacker looks to see where the defender is. To shield the ball the attacker should adopt the long barrier method and use their arms to feel if the defender is close.

The next coaching point we need to look at is the decision. Based on the defenders position can the attacker turn? Which turn will the attacker use to move the defender and enable them to get past?

The next coaching point is the technique of the turn itself. These are all the points we have looked at for each of the individual turns. The attacker should try to be clever and positive in turning the defender. As the coach you need to assess was the turn carried out correctly? If the attacker failed to get past the defender, why did they fail? What was wrong? Can you spot the problem and correct it?

The last point we need to check is that the end product or pass is accurate and weighted correctly. Not too fast that it is impossible to control, or so slow that it never gets there.

Make sure all the players participate in the drill as both the attacker and the defender.

Consider varying this drill what options can you come up with?

Instead of a player receiving at the opposite end of the channel put in a target goal. Now we can coach our attackers turning and shooting.

We can open the channel out into a larger 20x20 square and introduce another attacker and defender. Now we can coach passing and support.

*Coaching*the*Coach*

Now we have four players in the 20x20 square why don't we challenge both teams to attack when they get control of the ball. Eight players can be split into two teams. Either of the attackers can receive the ball off their server. They can then try to turn and pass the ball across the square to their receiver. If the other team intercepts the ball then they can try. They should pass the ball out to a server to start the drill and try to get the ball across the square. To promote turning the server cannot pass the ball directly across the square to the receiver, it has to go via a player in the square.

How can we create some fun?

We can award a goal for each time the ball gets from server via attacker to receiver. Which team is the first to three goals? Remember to swap the players in the middle so everyone gets a chance as the attacker.

Now we have moved on from coaching the specifics of the turns. We are now looking at a game environment, which promotes the use of a turn to beat a defender. As always assess the age and skill levels of your players. Which drill fits their ability levels and enables you to coach and improve them. Do they need to be coached the simple turn or are they now ready for a game related drill with defenders?

CoachingtheCoach -
Shooting

Shooting

Shooting 1 - "Target Ball"

Let's break down the action of shooting and discuss it briefly.

A shot is a powerful and accurate strike of a ball and therefore can be coached in the first instance much like a driven pass. A shot using the laces or centre of the top of the foot should strike through the centre of the ball.

We will need to breakdown the action of the shot in order that we can coach the key stages. Coach all four points in this logical order. Can you remember the different stages of a good pass? The stages of a good shot will be the same although the coaching points in each stage will be slightly different.

What were the key stages?

1.   Approach
2.   Body Shape
3.   Contact
4.   Follow through

Lets set up a simple drill to combine accuracy and power whilst giving the coach plenty of time and space to coach the correct technique of striking the ball. During this drill the coach can demonstrate each of the steps in turn and in a controlled environment.

The players should be split into pairs with one ball between them to use and one ball (the target ball) positioned between them on a disc or marker cone as in the diagram below.

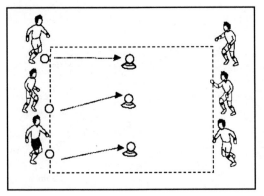

What distance should the players stand from the target ball? What would affect this distance?

If we take very young players or beginners they may not be able to strike the ball hard or accurately enough over any great distance. We therefore need to look at our players, assess their skill levels and set up the drill accordingly.

The two players are numbered 1 and 2. They then take turns in trying to kick their ball at the "target ball" and knock it off the cone.

They will need a shot or driven pass with accuracy and power to succeed. We can therefore use this drill to teach the key points of a good shot.

Would you just let all the players carry on alternately taking shots?

No. The drill will quickly dissolve into chaos if constant shots are taken. Players would be running about, collecting balls and running into the centre of the drill to reset the "target balls". Let us think about the drill and the requirements for good safe coaching.

The coach should be in control. All the player 1's down the left hand side of the diagram should take their shots on the coach's command. The balls can then be collected by the player 2's and lined up while the coach resets any target balls that have been knocked off. Only then when all is ready should the player 2's have their attempt, again on the coach's command, "shoot".

Now that the drill organisation is safe and working well we can begin to educate and coach the players.

What should we look for when our players take their shot, what are the points we can align to make sure the shot is accurate and powerful?

Go through the action of striking the ball in your head and consider the different stages of the shot. Remember how we broke down the coaching points.

Firstly for our shot we need to concentrate on the approach to the ball, which should be very slightly from the left side if striking the ball right footed and very slightly from the right side if striking with the left foot.

The body shape is always critical to a good shot. The standing foot should be planted right next to the side of the ball allowing the kicking foot to swing through. The head should be steady, knee over the ball and the arms out for balance. The standing foot should have the toes pointing in the direction of the shot so the whole body is in line.

The foot should then contact the ball with the laces of the boot kicking through the centre of the ball. This will mean that the ball goes straight along the ground.

The follow through should be short, but sharp and strong to keep the ball low and accurate. To maintain accuracy the follow through should be in the same direction as the shot.

Lets think now about how we should coach these points. Lets give the players the four pieces of information one at a time. Maybe after each couple of shots you could give them another piece of information to eventually complete the picture. Break down the shooting process coaching the four points in the logical order.

As the coach you can watch from the outside easily and clearly as each shot is taken when you permit and on your command.

If a shot misses wildly as the coach what question do you need to ask?

Why did it miss so badly? What did the player do wrong? Which of the four characteristics of a good shot was the missing point? Did you see what was performed wrongly? Can you question your players? Which part of the foot should they use? Laces. Can you explain to them what was wrong and demonstrate what is right? Can you coach?

How can we introduce some fun?

How about each of the player one's down the left hand side are Team A and any "target" ball knocked off the cone is a goal to them. Then Team B, the player two's down the right can have their turn and see how many goals they score. We now have a simple team game where accurate shots are rewarded with goals.

Can you use this simple drill for more advanced players? What would you change?

We can use this drill to coach our players to strike the ball cleanly and technically well so don't forget to coach them to strike the ball first with the right foot and then their left. They will need to be able to shoot with either foot in a game.

We can also make the distance to the target ball further and also change the size of the target ball. For younger players we may use a larger ball but remember the ball should not be too large that it is too heavy to easily be knocked off the cone.

Shooting 2 – Team Penalties

For our second drill we can incorporate a goal and three teams A, B and C. One target goal is placed in front of the teams and each team has their own ball placed in between them and the goal. Each of the team members can then line up ready to take their turn to shoot at goal.

The drill shown below has five players in each team. Upon the coach's command "Shoot" the first player from each of the 3 teams run up and strikes the ball at goal. That player then retrieves their ball, replaces it and rejoins the back of their team to await their next go.

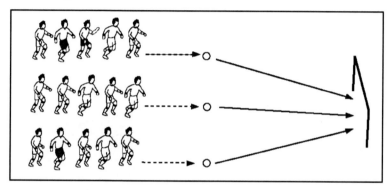

Let us now have a think about the organisation of the drill.

You are about to use the drill to coach a group of 5 and 6 year olds to shoot, how will this effect your organisation?

The target goal could be as big as six feet wide by four foot high or cones could be placed six feet apart.

The ball is placed a reasonable distance from the goal to suit the skill and strength of the players in relation to the size of the goal, in this age group it could be 6 to 12 yards away.

Coaching the Coach

Remember if the drill is too easy for your group of players amend it as you see fit during the session. In the picture above if every player keeps scoring we can amend the drill by moving the teams back further from the goal. We can even comment to the players how well they have done. So we are going to make it harder. How well can they do now, give your players a challenge.

What else might you change for better players?

1. Make the goals smaller.
2. Give 2 goals if they score and hit the side of the nets, this will promote shooting across the goal and into the corners.
3. Increase the angle for the shot from the wider two teams cones.
4. Switch the position of your teams so they all have to shoot from the different cones.
5. Only shoot with your weaker foot.
6. The players could throw the ball up themselves and practice volleys or half volleys.

The players should always retrieve their ball after their shot and replace the ball ready for the next player so leaving the coach free to supervise.

Do we need a goalkeeper?

No. Firstly there are 3 shots being taken so it would be unsafe to allow a goalkeeper. Secondly and more importantly for the younger players, we can let them shoot and score more often. This will promote a high success rate and sense of achievement. Everyone likes to score a goal.

As the coach you should encourage this and add fun as always. Ask the teams if they have scored yet and add competition by seeing which team is winning.

As the players take turns shooting, what will you coach and how will you coach it?

Remember the previous drill where we broke down the action of shooting into its separate parts. Reinforce these parts to make a technically sound shot at goal.

Can you remember the coaching points?

We should always coach them in the logical order that they are performed.

1.   Approach - The approach should be slightly from the side.
2.   Body Shape - The standing foot should be planted next to the side of the ball with the toe pointing at the goal. This allows the kicking foot to swing through with the head steady, knee over the ball and arms out for balance.
3.   Contact - The laces of the boot should contact the centre of the ball.
4.   Follow through - A short but sharp and strong follow through to keep the ball down and accurate in the direction of the shot.

These two drills can be fun and effective ways of coaching younger players. Lets move onto a drill, which can be used by all skill levels and introduces some competition.

Shooting 3 – Quick shooting

In this drill we can either use the penalty area as our playing zone, or mark out a square or rectangle. Each corner needs to be the same distance from the centre of the grid. On these corners we place our four teams and in the centre of one side of the playing area we put our goal. The goal can be anything from a full size goal to a small 4ft by 2ft target goal.

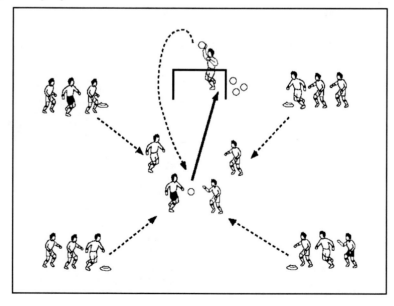

In the diagram on the opposite page, we have the four teams of three players and a target goal. For our younger inexperienced players we want lots of shots and goals. For better players you may want to add a goalkeeper.

The three players on each team are given a number from 1 to 3. The coach stands behind the goal with the ball and throws it into the playing area. At the same time they should shout one of the numbers. The player from each team that corresponds to the number called then runs into the playing area to get to the ball first and shoot at goal. Whenever a player scores a goal they score a goal for their team.

This drill is competitive as they are playing for themselves and their team. Speed is imperative not only to get to the ball first but also to shoot as quickly as possible and score a goal.

What will we coach?

In this drill we can always emphasise the key points we have discussed earlier that make up a good shot. If we see a bad shot we can stop the drill, go in and explain why it was a bad shot. Which key point was wrong? Did you spot the mistake? Demonstrate what and why and how you make it right.

We can also look at quick shooting, which foot would you use to shoot quickly and why?

In quick shooting our players have to use the foot nearest the ball. Players cannot afford to wait for the ball to come across their body to use their favourite foot. You will see younger players trying to run around the ball to enable a shot with their "best" foot. With other players around them the player needs to run directly at the ball to get their shot in with the nearest foot. If not, the ball will be simply taken from them. The players should not worry about their weaker or stronger foot. It is more important that the player has the right attitude, a belief that the player will score. If the player has the belief they will score then they often will.

What will you do if you have younger players?

We have already discussed not having a goalkeeper and the size of the goals to keep the success rate high. It would also be good to try and match the skill levels and sizes through the same numbered players of each team. We do not want one player scoring all the goals. We need to keep it challenging for all our players. Also we need to encourage our players to shoot at every opportunity. If they delay in taking a shot it is another opportunity for an opponent to recover and make another attempt to win back the ball. Finally keep the excitement and momentum high and encourage the players to shoot at every opportunity.

If you don't shoot, you will never score.

What will you do if you have better players?

1.   The size of the goals can be varied.
2.   More than one target goal, one each end or two on one side.
3.   We can add goalkeepers.
4.   We can shout more than one number so the players can work in pairs or shout which goal they have to score in.

Can we look at developing the current drill? It is originally a quick shooting drill but what else might you be able to coach?

What might you adapt this drill to coach?

With better more skilful players you may want to also coach dribbling, taking on and beating opponents or executing turns to enable a shot.

What mistakes do you think you might see in this drill and be able to address and coach?

1. Did the player kick the ball too far ahead of them giving an opportunity to the defender to pinch the ball?
2. Did they fail trying to beat the defender; was the "move" or turn not technically correct?

Spot the mistake, stop the play and explain why you stopped them. Explain and demonstrate what went wrong. Ask them if they have any comments or suggestions. Do they have the answer and can they show you? Demonstrate correctly and coach them.

We can also use this drill to coach striking partnerships. We can shout two numbers and have two players from each team. This means we can look at one two's and clever play between partners. The coaching opportunities are endless.

Remember with this drill we can coach a number of different things be it the original concept of quick shooting, dribbling and taking on opponents, turns or even goalkeeping. This is why we need to plan ahead. Prepare a session plan and list the coaching points that we want to achieve from the drill. Concentrate on one theme and coach all the key stages or points in the logical sequence.

We have now looked at three easy shooting drills. These can be used to coach the basic points leading to a good shot or shooting in a game related competitive environment.

Let us see how we can take what we have learnt and use it with other coaching books. Select another shooting drill. What does it lend itself to coaching? Is it a simple drill where you can easily break down the key stages of a good shot and coach them? Is it for a lone striker or winger to practice against defenders or are we beginning to look at playing in pairs? Is it an intricate drill where you need to find space for a shot by turning the opposition or quick clever play?

Don't just pick any drill from any book and use it. Break it down into stages and look at how you can use it and most importantly what it helps you to coach.

*Coaching*the*Coach -*
Heading

Heading

Heading 1 – Your Players First Header

This first heading drill in the chapter is aimed very much at our very young or new footballers. It is a drill we can use to give them the confidence and sense of achievement to begin to head the ball.

For younger players we start with our players in pairs and kneeling opposite each other about two feet apart. Older players may want to start further apart and standing. One coach can quite comfortably manage about eight pairs. Each pair should kneel about three feet apart giving themselves plenty of room, see diagram below.

Number the players 1 and 2. Player 1 holds the ball lightly with both hands either side of the ball and with the ball at the same height as their forehead. The player then brings the ball back toward their forehead slowly with their hands and heads through the centre of the ball to their partner.

Player 2 then catches the ball and repeats the process heading the ball back to player 1.

This drill can continue looping, be aware of the amount of time taken, they should only have three or four headers and then relax.

Because they bring the ball onto their own head they can control the speed and impact. This means they can get comfortable heading the ball before they progress.

g 2 – Heading Trios

ers have learnt all the fundamentals of heading we can move forward
simple drill. In this drill we have three players lined up with four or five
them, dependent upon ability and size. We can have four or five sets of
ayers lined up, but again we need to keep five feet between them as a
e ball should be thrown underarm from player 1 to player 2 in the
ould then head it backwards to player 3 behind them.

be repeated with player 3 throwing to player 2 to head back to player 1
eryone gets three or four attempts as the player in the middle.

ou going to coach them during these three or four headers?

go over the basics again. They need to keep their mouths shut and their
atching the ball. Head the ball, do not let the ball head you. This time though
look at the contact of the forehead on the ball to enable the player to flick
The player should be leaning or jumping slightly backward to enable the top
ead to get a slight touch underneath the centre of the ball sending it
kwards.

ou progress this drill?

vith player 1 heading the ball to player 2 who then heads it on for player 3
ayer 3 can then begin the drill again heading the ball to player 2 who flicks
olayer 1 to catch. We can progress this further by trying to keep the ball
ough continuous headers. Player 1 heads to 2 who then heads to 3 who
to 2 who then heads it back to 1 and it all starts again.

ou create some fun?

For health and safety reasons we should always monitor how long we use heading drills, especially with younger less experienced players. We do not want them continually heading the ball. You should also check the size and weight of the footballs being used. If you have younger players do not use adult footballs. The FA has recommended sizes of footballs for all ages so please use the correct balls. It is far better to coach a few good headers than leave them to twenty minutes continuous heading.

What are you going to coach during these three or four headers?

Before they even start to practice make sure they know a header is undertaken by hitting the centre of the ball with the forehead. Demonstrate the technique. Ask the players, should they have their eyes open? Yes. Why? So the players can always see the ball.

What would you tell players about their mouth?

The mouth should be closed when heading the ball. If it is open the tongue can get trapped between the teeth and bitten by the player.

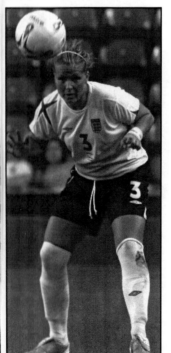

Make sure everyone is comfortable and balanced, eyes open, mouth closed and heading with the forehead through the centre of the ball. Make the players aware that they should head the ball and not let the ball head them, or hit them.

Now we can move on or increase the difficulty of the drill. You can go straight to any level of this drill dependant on what you have done before with your players and how comfortable they are heading the ball.

Simply get the players to stand instead of kneeling and repeat the process. The players can try another three or four headers bringing the ball back slowly in their hands onto their foreheads.

What are the points we need to remember?

Mouth shut, eyes open and use the forehead to head through the centre of the ball. Head the ball do not let the ball head you. Coach and inform your players.

To progress this drill we move from the ball in the hands to a lightly thrown ball. Player I should lightly throw the ball up into the air and then head it to player 2. Again the player heading the ball is in control of the drill and their own header. They can throw it up higher the more confident they become.

Again player 2 can then repeat the process and head it back to player I and continue. Remember, only three or four precise headers each.

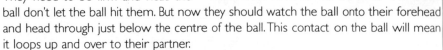

What point would you change for this variation?

The players still need to have their mouths shut and eyes open. They need to be firm and head the ball don't let the ball hit them. But now they should watch the ball onto their forehead and head through just below the centre of the ball. This contact on the ball will mean it loops up and over to their partner.

What might you do or say to better players?

Better players will need to stand further apart. Let's be bigger, braver and more positive. The coach can begin to explain about using the upper body to provide more power as the head is pushed forward to contact the ball. The player should push the forehead forward and their arms back.

We can progress this drill again. Up to now the player heading the ball has always been in control of the ball and the challenge. Now we will change it so that player I lightly throws the ball, underarm into the air, for player 2 to head back to them. Again monitor the players. The players are likely to pull out of the header or turn away as they are not in control of the pace of the ball. Give each player a couple of goes then switch so each player can take their turn.

What might you do or say to younger players?

Build your players confidence with lots of praise and encouragement. Remember the key points, explain them and demonstrate. Always try to stop on a positive to leave them with the sense of success.

What might you do or say to better players?

When throwing the ball player I should tell player 2 to head it back either "High" or "Low". Player I shouts "High" or "Low" and then throws the ball.

What points do you need to change?

When the player shouts "High" the player needs to head through the underneath of the centre of the ball to project the ball up. If the player shouts "Low" the contact has to be above the centre of the ball to direct it downward. The players may even have to jump up or stoop down to enable their forehead to contact the correct part of the ball.

What might you do to add some fun?

Everyone loves a diving header. Demonstrate diving f to a partner coach. Make it look fun and exciting. Get Remember to only try three or four attempts each an header. Do not try a diving header on unsuitable surfac astro turf pitches. Always make sure it is a safe environ

Remember to be positive when coaching heading and Don't attempt too much too quickly. Always try and finis with a sense of achievement.

Now our pla onto anothe feet betweer these three safety area. middle who

This can the Make sure e

What are

We need t eyes open we need to it backwar of the for looping ba

How can

Let's start to catch. it back to rotating t heads bac

How can

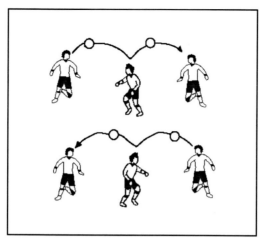

A simple relay race could be used to inject some fun. The first team to head the ball out to player 3 and back again to player 1. You could also put the players into two teams, so instead of three players in line you may have six. The same idea is used to head the ball from player 1 onto player 2 then 3 and so on until it gets all the way to player number 6 who catches the ball and sprints back to the front of the line to win.

How can we make the drill more competitive?

Go back to the original drill with the three players and put an opponent against the player in the middle that is heading the ball?

Heading 3 – Throw-Head-Catch

For this drill we move back into a 20x20 square again and split our group into two teams. The teams have to get the ball from one side of the square to the other by using a throw, head, and catch sequence.

This means the first player throws the ball to a teammate who then has to head the ball onto another third teammate. The third player can then catch it and throw it again. So the ball moves via throw, head, catch, throw, head, and catch across the square.

The other team can steal the ball when the opponents next move is to catch the ball by jumping up and catching it before their opponents catch it. They can then try to get the ball over the other end line. If a team gets the ball over the end line then they score a goal.

Now we have a very simple drill where players are jumping and heading the ball but under pressure. It will also improve direction as they have to head to a teammate. As this drill involves lots of movement, jumping and stretching it could also be used as a warm up drill.

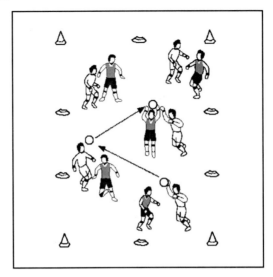

Can we progress this drill?

We could incorporate a goal at each end line. This means we have moved the drill on from simply heading over an end line to heading to score. This will force the players into the two heading types. The heading up and away, a defensive type header and the heading down, an attacking header.

These are very basic and simple heading drills but any heading drill you find can be used as long as you follow the simple rules. Do not have your players heading hundreds of balls all session long. Rotate your players so everyone gets their turn. Concentrate on a few technically sound headers. Continue to instil the coaching points we have discussed. Mouth shut, eyes open, contact point on ball with forehead. Most importantly leave your players with positive results and sense of achievement.

For health and safety reasons we should always monitor how long we use heading drills, especially with younger less experienced players. We do not want them continually heading the ball. You should also check the size and weight of the footballs being used. If you have younger players do not use adult footballs. The FA has recommended sizes of footballs for all ages so please use the correct balls. It is far better to coach a few good headers than leave them to twenty minutes continuous heading.

What are you going to coach during these three or four headers?

Before they even start to practice make sure they know a header is undertaken by hitting the centre of the ball with the forehead. Demonstrate the technique. Ask the players, should they have their eyes open? Yes. Why? So the players can always see the ball.

What would you tell players about their mouth?

The mouth should be closed when heading the ball. If it is open the tongue can get trapped between the teeth and bitten by the player.

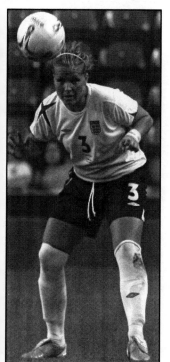

Make sure everyone is comfortable and balanced, eyes open, mouth closed and heading with the forehead through the centre of the ball. Make the players aware that they should head the ball and not let the ball head them, or hit them.

Now we can move on or increase the difficulty of the drill. You can go straight to any level of this drill dependant on what you have done before with your players and how comfortable they are heading the ball.

Simply get the players to stand instead of kneeling and repeat the process. The players can try another three or four headers bringing the ball back slowly in their hands onto their foreheads.

What are the points we need to remember?

Mouth shut, eyes open and use the forehead to head through the centre of the ball. Head the ball do not let the ball head you. Coach and inform your players.

To progress this drill we move from the ball in the hands to a lightly thrown ball. Player 1 should lightly throw the ball up into the air and then head it to player 2. Again the player heading the ball is in control of the drill and their own header. They can throw it up higher the more confident they become.

Again player 2 can then repeat the process and head it back to player 1 and continue. Remember, only three or four precise headers each.

What point would you change for this variation?

The players still need to have their mouths shut and eyes open. They need to be firm and head the ball don't let the ball hit them. But now they should watch the ball onto their forehead and head through just below the centre of the ball. This contact on the ball will mean it loops up and over to their partner.

What might you do or say to better players?

Better players will need to stand further apart. Let's be bigger, braver and more positive. The coach can begin to explain about using the upper body to provide more power as the head is pushed forward to contact the ball. The player should push the forehead forward and their arms back.

We can progress this drill again. Up to now the player heading the ball has always been in control of the ball and the challenge. Now we will change it so that player 1 lightly throws the ball, underarm into the air, for player 2 to head back to them. Again monitor the players. The players are likely to pull out of the header or turn away as they are not in control of the pace of the ball. Give each player a couple of goes then switch so each player can take their turn.

What might you do or say to younger players?

Build your players confidence with lots of praise and encouragement. Remember the key points, explain them and demonstrate. Always try to stop on a positive to leave them with the sense of success.

What might you do or say to better players?

When throwing the ball player 1 should tell player 2 to head it back either "High" or "Low". Player 1 shouts "High" or "Low" and then throws the ball.

What points do you need to change?

When the player shouts "High" the player needs to head through the underneath of the centre of the ball to project the ball up. If the player shouts "Low" the contact has to be above the centre of the ball to direct it downward. The players may even have to jump up or stoop down to enable their forehead to contact the correct part of the ball.

What might you do to add some fun?

Everyone loves a diving header. Demonstrate diving forward and heading the ball back to a partner coach. Make it look fun and exciting. Get the players to try for themselves. Remember to only try three or four attempts each and coach the key points of a good header. Do not try a diving header on unsuitable surfaces such as indoor gyms' or some astro turf pitches. Always make sure it is a safe environment for the practice.

Remember to be positive when coaching heading and slowly increase the difficulty. Don't attempt too much too quickly. Always try and finish the drill leaving your players with a sense of achievement.

Heading 2 – Heading Trios

Now our players have learnt all the fundamentals of heading we can move forward onto another simple drill. In this drill we have three players lined up with four or five feet between them, dependent upon ability and size. We can have four or five sets of these three players lined up, but again we need to keep five feet between them as a safety area. The ball should be thrown underarm from player 1 to player 2 in the middle who should then head it backwards to player 3 behind them.

This can then be repeated with player 3 throwing to player 2 to head back to player 1. Make sure everyone gets three or four attempts as the player in the middle.

What are you going to coach them during these three or four headers?

We need to go over the basics again. They need to keep their mouths shut and their eyes open watching the ball. Head the ball, do not let the ball head you. This time though we need to look at the contact of the forehead on the ball to enable the player to flick it backward. The player should be leaning or jumping slightly backward to enable the top of the forehead to get a slight touch underneath the centre of the ball sending it looping backwards.

How can you progress this drill?

Let's start with player 1 heading the ball to player 2 who then heads it on for player 3 to catch. Player 3 can then begin the drill again heading the ball to player 2 who flicks it back to player 1 to catch. We can progress this further by trying to keep the ball rotating through continuous headers. Player 1 heads to 2 who then heads to 3 who heads back to 2 who then heads it back to 1 and it all starts again.

How can you create some fun?

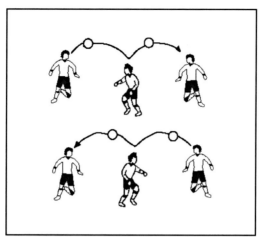

A simple relay race could be used to inject some fun. The first team to head the ball out to player 3 and back again to player 1. You could also put the players into two teams, so instead of three players in line you may have six. The same idea is used to head the ball from player 1 onto player 2 then 3 and so on until it gets all the way to player number 6 who catches the ball and sprints back to the front of the line to win.

How can we make the drill more competitive?

Go back to the original drill with the three players and put an opponent against the player in the middle that is heading the ball?

Heading 3 – Throw-Head-Catch

For this drill we move back into a 20x20 square again and split our group into two teams. The teams have to get the ball from one side of the square to the other by using a throw, head, and catch sequence.

This means the first player throws the ball to a teammate who then has to head the ball onto another third teammate. The third player can then catch it and throw it again. So the ball moves via throw, head, catch, throw, head, and catch across the square.

The other team can steal the ball when the opponents next move is to catch the ball by jumping up and catching it before their opponents catch it. They can then try to get the ball over the other end line. If a team gets the ball over the end line then they score a goal.

Now we have a very simple drill where players are jumping and heading the ball but under pressure. It will also improve direction as they have to head to a teammate. As this drill involves lots of movement, jumping and stretching it could also be used as a warm up drill.

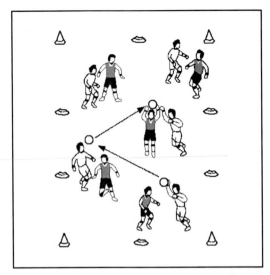

Can we progress this drill?

We could incorporate a goal at each end line. This means we have moved the drill on from simply heading over an end line to heading to score. This will force the players into the two heading types. The heading up and away, a defensive type header and the heading down, an attacking header.

These are very basic and simple heading drills but any heading drill you find can be used as long as you follow the simple rules. Do not have your players heading hundreds of balls all session long. Rotate your players so everyone gets their turn. Concentrate on a few technically sound headers. Continue to instil the coaching points we have discussed. Mouth shut, eyes open, contact point on ball with forehead. Most importantly leave your players with positive results and sense of achievement.

*Coaching*the*Coach* - *Goalkeeping*

Goalkeeping

Goalkeeping 1 – Handling

Which player suffers most when we plan our sessions? Do we ever prepare a session for our goalkeepers?

All young players love to go in goal at one time or another so make sure all your young players get the chance to play and be coached in this position. We don't know which player will ultimately become a striker or a defender so how do we know who will mature into a goalkeeper. With this in mind let us make sure we dedicate a team training session to the basics of goalkeeping every so often.

This drill is a simple but effective way to coach a series of goalkeeping points. Before we start the drill make sure the players are using the correct size ball for their age. For younger players you may need to use size 3 balls. In this drill we first get our players into pairs (player 1 and 2) and allocate them a channel each, 5 feet wide by about 10 feet long. See diagram below.

Player 1 rolls the ball along the floor to player 2. Player 2 then crouches down receiving the ball, picks it up with both hands, and brings it into the chest.

Player 2 rolls it back to player 1 so they can pick up the ball and repeat the process. Promote the use of both hands rolling the ball first with the right and then the left hand. An easy drill to let the goalkeepers get a feel of the ball, stop it and pick it up.

What will you coach?

We need to first look at our player's body position, or "Set Position". This is the position the goalkeeper should adopt immediately prior to a shot.

Our goalkeepers need to have their legs apart for balance but not too far apart. A good guideline is to have the feet in line with the shoulders. Why? If they have them too far apart the ball can go through their legs. It also promotes lots of small steps when moving sideways instead of large strides. A goalkeeper cannot dive if their legs are wide apart. We should also promote bent knees, standing on the balls of the feet and fingers facing the ball. The goalkeeper should also be leaning forward a good trigger phrase for them to remember is "Nose over Toes". Most importantly concentrate on the ball and be alert.

We can now specifically look at the two ways our goalkeepers can collect the ball. They can use the "K" position, which is shown on the left. This is where the knee is positioned next to the ankle of the other foot. This provides a long barrier to the ball as shown. The goalkeeper could also reach straight down, shown below right. The legs and feet are placed roughly 3/4 of the ball width apart. Note in both cases the legs are behind the ball and there is no gap for the ball to go through.

Can you think of a way to progress this drill?

We should start to let the players roll the ball slightly to the side of our goalkeepers. The goalkeepers now have to move into line with the ball before picking it up. They should move sideways with small steps but keep their body and eyes facing the ball. We can of course start to roll the ball faster and further away. Remember to base the difficulty on the skill level of your players. Can they cope? If not make it easier and promote success and confidence.

We can now move onto catching the ball. Player 1 should throw the ball into player 2's chest. Player 2 can repeat the drill throwing the ball back into player 1's chest. Vary the distance between the players dependant on their ability.

What are you looking to coach?

We need to look at the "Set Position" of our goalkeepers before we move onto the technique of catching the ball.

What did we say, could you list the points?

1.   The goalkeeper should be on their toes with their fingers pointing at the ball.
2.   The goalkeeper should be leaning slightly forward, "Nose over Toes"
3.   They should have their "Feet in line with their Shoulders".
4.   The goalkeeper should be alert and watching the ball.

Demonstrate the position you want, stable, balanced and alert.

Now let's look at the type of catch they should be making. When the ball is thrown into them they should cup their arms underneath the ball with their hands at the front and roll the ball up into the chest.

Should we credit a goalkeeper for catching the ball in front of their waist with their palms facing the ball or slightly downward?

No, the ball could be dropped easily straight down unlike when the ball is cupped and supported by the arms. Demonstrate what could happen and why you want them to cup the ball.

We can progress again with the players still in pairs. The players now throw the ball slightly higher at head height. This means the goalkeeper has to catch the ball in front of their face.

What is important to coach and explain?

To catch the ball at this height we use the "W" technique. This is shown below. Note that the fingers are splayed out to grip around the ball while the thumbs are kept together. The goalkeepers should watch the ball all the way into their hands. They should never close their eyes.

Why do we need the thumbs together?

If the thumbs are apart the ball can slip through the hands and into the goalkeepers face or the goal. The goalkeeper needs this protection to catch the ball cleanly and safely. Demonstrate the 'W' position to the players with your hands and show the thumbs together.

What might you do for more experienced goalkeepers?

In all these drills our players have thrown the ball for our goalkeepers to save. We can move onto catching a kicked ball. With players kicking the ball it means the ball will be moving much faster. With the introduction of kicking the ball we can also test our goalkeepers further by aiming further to the sides. This will progress the drill and introduce our goalkeepers to diving saves.

When we move onto diving saves can we stress the need to catch the ball. The goalkeeper should lead with both hands and have their hands close together. You could even use the example of imagining they are handcuffed together, keeping the 'W' position. Challenge your goalkeepers can they catch it?

Remember, this is a drill for a goalkeeper. Is there any benefit to a player smashing the ball past the goalkeeper every time? No. The players should strike the ball firmly but so the goalkeeper is tested, not stranded.

Which type of catch have we not looked at?

We can use the same format for the players to throw the ball high to their partners so they can jump up and catch the ball. This will simulate jumping to catch a cross in a game.

What can we coach?

With the high jumping catch let us think about the jump especially the take off. If we take off from one foot we will get higher. We can also ask our players to use their arms to swing up giving more momentum. In a game they should raise the knee of the leg furthest from the goal or nearest the strikers. This will give protection against any striker challenging for the ball. This means they will need to practice jumping for the ball whilst raising each knee alternately.

Can we think of any other drills we have seen before in this book, which could be used for our goalkeepers?

The shooting drill "Quick Shooting" could be used for coaching the goalkeepers. We can also use the heading drill "Throw Head Catch".

What would you look to coach in these drills?

For the "Quick Shooting" drill assess the "Set Position" of the goalkeeper before a shot is taken. The goalkeeper should stay in line with the ball as it moves about the square taking small steps to the side. This means they are always positioned in line with the ball and the centre of the goal. They should keep their eyes fixed on the ball and body square. They should get set as the attackers foot is drawn back for a shot.

The goalkeeper's basic handling and shot stopping can then be coached. If the shot is low then we can coach the "K" position. A shot into the body and we can look at the goalkeepers "Cup" technique. A high shot will allow us to coach the "W" position of the hands and the jump of the goalkeeper. Did they raise their knee and was it the correct one? The knee raised should be the one nearest the attackers for protection.

In the "Throw Head Catch" drill we need to focus on handling especially the "W" position of the hands. This is especially useful for promoting jumping to catch the ball under pressure and the raising of the nearest leg for protection.

Goalkeeping 2 – Goalie Wars

This is a great 1 v 1 drill for two goalkeepers and can become very competitive. The set up is for each goalkeeper to defend a five yard wide goal with the goals ten yards apart.

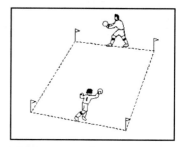

Each goalkeeper has a ball and on the coach's command throws the ball at their opposite goalkeepers goal trying to score.

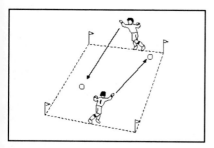

Once they have thrown the balls they must react quickly to save the throw from their opponent. The throw is limited to the standard goalkeeping throws. The roll, the side arm, the javelin or the over arm throw. Once they have saved the ball they wait for the coach's command and the next simultaneous throw and save. Any goal scored gains the goalkeeper a point.

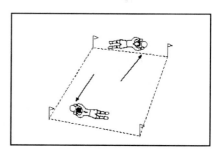

What can we coach?

Firstly we can coach all four of the throws independently.

Look at the picture sequences and make sure you can perform the throws yourself, as you will need to demonstrate them to your players.

*Coaching*the*Coach*

For the Roll out we can promote the underarm bowling type action. A low body and extended arm rolls the ball underarm. Make sure the ball goes along the ground fairly quickly and accurately.

For the Side arm we promote being side on and with a wide stance. The goalkeeper slings the ball at hip / chest height.

With the Javelin we need a wide base and the ball is thrown with an open palm from the chest / shoulder. The trajectory of the throw is more downward than the side arm throw.

The Over-arm throw uses a wider stance again and leading with the opposite hand we use a cricket bowling type action to propel the ball.

We can now move onto coaching quick reactions.

The goalkeepers should be alert as soon as their own throw is released. The goalkeeper should get in line with their opponents ball as soon as possible. They should also get into the "Set" position as early as possible.

What would you think if the goalkeeper were alert, but jumping on the goal line?

If the goalkeeper is jumping they will lose valuable reaction time, as they must wait until they touch the floor again to dive. A goalkeeper who is set with the balls of their feet on the ground will always be able to react quicker as they can dive immediately.

How can we make this drill more challenging?

For the older or better players you can continually rotate the throws and saves without extra commands.

The drill is again started on the coach's order to throw. Both keepers throw but this time, as soon as the goalkeeper saves their opponents shot they can throw again. They do not have to wait until the coach's order. This will raise the tempo of the drill and the goalkeepers will need to increase their speed and agility to deal with the continuing throws. We can still have one point awarded for each goal scored.

Once you have increased the tempo and their reaction speeds we can progress the drill again by giving the goalkeepers the option to kick. This will make the shots harder and more demanding to save.

Goalkeeping 3 – Shot Stopping

In this drill the players are set out as in the diagram below. Obviously we now understand that the area is dependant upon the skill levels and age of the players taking part.

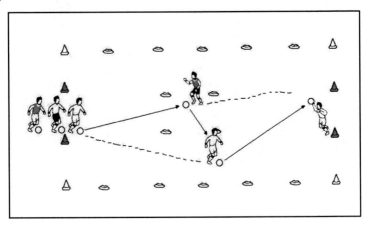

In this drill we have our goalkeeper positioned in a goal at one end of the coned area. A line of players, with a ball each, waits at the other end. On the coaches command the first player in the queue passes the ball into the player in the coned square. This player can then lay the ball off to the first player who has continued their run to shoot. The player in the square should follow in the shot. The player who has taken the shot replaces the player in the square and the player following in the shot returns to the back of the queue. It is important that the player rejoins the back of the queue by walking all the way around the drill area with their ball and not through it. The drill can then be repeated safely and more quickly,

Why does the player in the square follow in the shot?

The player is adding pressure onto the goalkeeper to make a clean save and hold onto the ball. If the goalkeeper spills the ball then the player is there to take a second shot from any rebound. This means we can test and coach our goalkeeper to react quickly to any drops or spills.

What else can we coach?

Lets think back to all the things we have talked about already.

The goalkeeper should get into the set position just as the player is about to shoot. They should be on their toes, not jumping and with their fingers pointing at the ball. The goalkeeper should be leaning slightly forward with, 'Nose over Toes' and 'Feet in line with their Shoulders'. They should be alert and watching the ball.

We can then use the drill to coach any technical information about the 'W' technique or the 'Cup' save for example.

What else could we add?

We need to coach the positioning of the goalkeeper prior to the shot being taken. If the shot is coming in from the right then the goalkeeper needs to position themselves off their line and slightly to the right to 'Narrow the angle'. This makes the goalkeeper appear bigger and gives the striker less of a target to aim for. Remember the goalkeeper must know where their goal is. If they are moving into position they should always take a look over their shoulder to see where the goal is and their relative position to it and the ball.

The goalkeeper should move into position quickly with small steps. Why? So they are always in close contact with the ground and therefore in a position to dive. Also it means they are less likely to cross their legs. Why is this important? Stand up now and cross your legs can you dive? No, it's impossible until you uncross your legs wasting more time. Why should the player in the square be encouraged to lay off both to the right and left? This means the goalkeeper will have to change positions relative to where the shot is taken and return to the centre of the goal after each shot.

How can we create some fun?

Lets give the attackers a point for every goal but give the goalkeeper a point for every save or shot off target.

Now we can duplicate the drill so all our squad are more actively involved, including our reserve goalkeeper. Simply set up the same drill to run parallel.

We can now coach our two goalkeepers on their positioning, the set position, their shot stopping technique and most importantly give them valuable shot stopping practice.

Because we have set up two independent drills we can also add competition. As before we can have points for players who score and points for goalkeepers who save shots. Now though we can add competition through the two goalkeepers keeping score against each other and also the two teams of players scoring against each other.

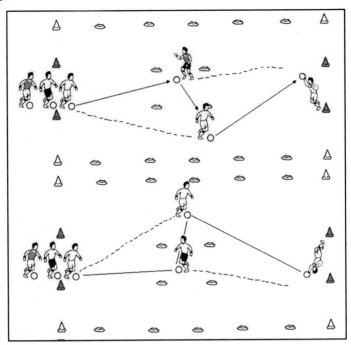

How can we increase the challenge and intensity?

Simply let the drill last for a set time. Let them play for one minute, how many saves and how many goals. Then we can swap the goalkeepers over so they face the other team of players. How did they do this time? How did they do against the other Goalkeepers score? How did they do against their own last score?

This drill also gives us the opportunity to coach many other skills.

We could use the drill to coach shooting. What would you coach? Look where the goalkeeper is before shooting with the laces of the nearest foot. We could also coach a lofted pass into the player in the square and the technique of the lay off. The ball must go in front of the player at a comfortable speed to enable a direct run and first time shot.

This drill will give our goalkeepers valuable shot stopping practice in a very intense and competitive environment. Remember to plan your sessions and coach your goalkeeper. As you can see from this drill everyone can be made to enjoy the goalkeeping session.

Coaching the Coach -
Games

Games

Games

At the end of every coaching session we finish with a game, after all it's what they have been asking for since the start. No matter what age they are.

It is very important to let players run with the ball and try out new tricks or skills within a game environment, especially the younger players. It is equally as important to introduce all players to the different positions within the team and highlight their own specific demands.

Our younger players, 7 and 8 year olds, will soon begin playing Mini-Soccer (7 a-side). So let us think about the game we are going to play at the end of our coaching session. How can we use this game to coach and educate our players? First we will need to assess our players and decide what we want to coach.

Can you think of any issues or coaching points you have seen with very young teams and players within a game?

Let's think about young or new players who all run around the pitch chasing the ball? We have all seen it when the ball becomes encircled by a swarm of frantic six year olds all trying to get a toe to the ball.

What do you think we need to do?

How can we teach our player's about positions and get them ready for mini soccer? What are the defensive third, the midfield and the attacking third? How can we get some organisation and team shape with players so young or inexperienced?

Games I – Third's Game

Let us add some rules to our game. How about splitting our pitch into three areas by adding two lines of different coloured cones.

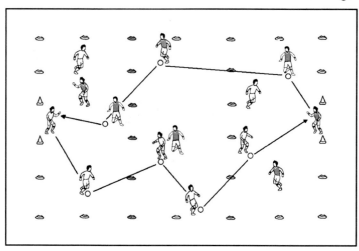

As you can see from the diagram above we now have three clear sections. These are: the defensive, midfield and attacking thirds.

With the pitch clearly split, the players are given specific rules. Defenders can only play within the defensive third, a midfielder must stay within the midfield third and the attackers cannot move out of the attacking third.

Now we have a team structure and we can put our players in our preferred seven a-side formation. We have chosen 2,3,1 as in the diagram above. As the coach you may want to change your formations and see how it affects the game.

Now we are starting to organise our team shape and introduce players to the requirements of different positions. With a structure to our team we can begin to coach other areas of the game.

What might you coach easily in a third's game?

Passing is the obvious skill to coach during this drill. We can coach the specific technical points of a good pass but also creating space and receiving skills. Look back at Passing 2 – Passing 3 v 1 and read again. Refresh yourself of all the points and skills to coach.

We can also coach Turns, Shooting and Goalkeeping easily within this drill. Coach the specific points logically as discussed in the earlier chapters.

How can you coach during the game?

Remember our 'Stop Stand Still' command? We can use this short sharp command to stop the players on the pitch at the time you see a problem. Spotting the problem early and stopping the game is key to coaching. This will improve as you become more experienced.

Coaching the Coach

Lets think about our third's game and the fact that we are coaching passing. If nobody has moved to create space and therefore the player with the ball has no option to pass, immediately stop the game. 'Stop Stand Still' Now the players are positioned exactly at the time a problem occurs. Now we can coach them, ask them why we have stopped the game, what can they do?

We are coaching passing and creating space so ask them where can they move, how should they move. Go into the game and take the place of the player you want to coach. Demonstrate the movement to create the space. Can they make a late and fast run off the

defender to receive the ball in space and half turned? Can they hold up the defender to receive the ball to feet? Show them the options.

If you are coaching turns you should stop the game when the player with the ball has an opportunity to turn a defender and does not attempt it or fails trying. Promote the fact that this opportunity has arisen within the game and get them to try and turn. Coach the technical points of a good turn. If you are

coaching shooting and a player misses with a shot, again stop the game. Coach the technique of the shot, why it missed, demonstrate and let the player have another attempt. Remember always finish with success to promote the sense of achievement.

Would you coach all these skills in one session?

We have seen that we need to select a specific drill and concentrate on what we want to coach our players. In the same way we should go on from the drill and reiterate the same theme through the game. If our session consists of a warm up, passing drill, and game, we then concentrate on passing skills during the game. This way we can take what we have learnt in the drill and take it into a game environment.

How could we develop passing for older players?

Firstly we could add more movement. The midfielder who makes the pass into our forward could follow the pass into the attacking third to add support, as they would in a game. Only the midfielder who makes the pass can move forward. This is shown by the dotted line in the diagram below.

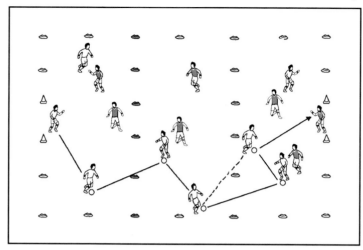

This means we develop our game to look at either one-two passes or our striker holding the ball up for a lay off. Coach the wide barrier to hold back the defender to enable a pass into feet. We can then coach the long barrier to keep the ball out of the defenders reach or the flick round the corner to play the one two.

This game could be used to coach counter attacking by developing quick passing and playing at speed. We could also include longer passes cutting out the midfield. With counter attacking we can also concentrate on our goalkeepers distribution and the need to release the ball quickly and accurately.

Going back to our younger players, we have looked at our team shape and structure. Our players can now begin to understand their roles within the team and the need to spread out. But we also have to promote dribbling skills and running with the ball. We need to let players express themselves and try things out.

This game does not really promote wing play or dribbling so we need to change the organisation to develop these skills.

Consider how you can amend the current game to incorporate wing play and dribbling?

Games 2 – Wing Game

In this game we simply amend the organisation so we can promote the use of wing play and dribbling. We change the position of the cones by removing the thirds. We use the different coloured cones to create wing channels on each side of the pitch. We also need to put in a half way line.

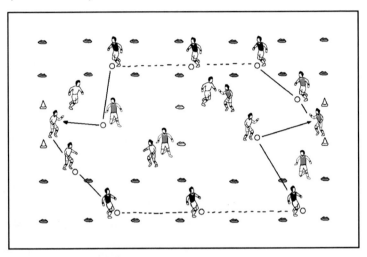

The two teams line up with three defenders and a goalkeeper in their own half, and two attackers in the opponents half. There is also a neutral winger (shown wearing a black bib) in each of the wing channels.

We now need some rules. The ball cannot be played from the defensive half directly into the attacking half. The ball has to be played out to either of the neutral wingers by a defender. The winger then dribbles the ball along the channel unopposed and crosses it back into a striker in the attacking half.

Remember to give everyone a chance to play as the winger.

What can we coach in the wing's game?

Obviously we can coach the wingers running with the ball or dribbling. But we also need to concentrate on the defenders looking for a pass to their winger and the winger being in a position to receive the pass. The winger cannot let an attacker position themselves between them and the defender with the ball. Why? The defender will not be able to pass the ball to them as the attacker is in the way.

We can then coach the cross back into the attacker. Do we want a high cross, a low cross or a cut back?

From this we can go on to coaching the striker's run and the timing of the run, late and fast to get away from the defenders. These are all things we can coach but with younger players concentrate on one theme and coach one theme only.

So if our session concentrated on creating space then during the game we are looking to coach players to create space. Is the winger in a position to receive the ball? Are they an outlet for our defenders? If not, ask them why not. Explain why and demonstrate what would be better and how.

We can use the same drill or game many times but remember to be clear what you want to use it for and what you want to coach.

Can we progress this drill?

As it stands the game will enable the winger to run with the ball more than dribble. Running with the ball means they will take bigger kicks in between touches and sprint unopposed after the ball. This encourages the player to exploit the space in front of them and is the correct option.

If we want our players to concentrate more on dribbling and the skills needed to beat an opponent, we will need to adapt the game.

What might you do?

We can put two players, one from each team into both channels. Now our players have to compete and take on their opponent 1 v 1. Shown in the top channel of the diagram below.

It maybe necessary to make sure the winger can receive the ball from the defenders unopposed. For this to happen the wingers should remain in their own half of the pitch waiting for the pass. Only when they receive the ball can they carry it over the half way line and attempt to beat the opposing player.

This may still prove difficult for some players. You might want to start with a couple of cones to dribble round just like the simple dribbling drill earlier in the book. This is shown in the bottom channel of the diagram below. The cones should be placed at the half way line to enable it to be used by the neutral player going both ways.

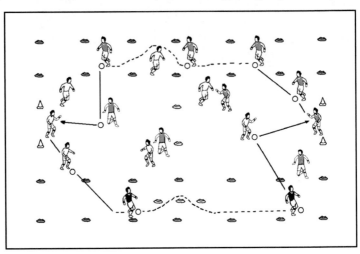

Remember to allow an amount of time for coaching mixed with free time in a game. We need our players to try new things and express themselves. There is an obvious importance for a team and its players to understand roles and formations and not all chase around after one ball. It is equally important we do not create robot players. We need flair and creativity in our young players and we should encourage it and give them every opportunity to try something different.

Mix these games up. Try a few minutes with rules and coaching to reiterate what you have coached during the session then let them play. Do not keep stopping the game, wait for the mistake and pick the time to coach. If you continually stop the game the players will loose interest and more importantly stop listening. Make sure you allow time for free play, no rules. See if they have learnt what you have coached but also give them time to experiment and try new things.

*Coaching*the*Coach* - Planning a Session

Planning a Coaching Session

The primary concern of any coach or club is the health and safety of the players and coaches they are responsible for. So before we start to consider and plan our session we need to think about our players and any health and safety issues.

What do you think we need to address in terms of the health and safety of players and coaches during the session?

Before any coach can begin a training session or game it is imperative that a number of checks are made to ensure a safe environment. The training ground or pitch should always be thoroughly checked for hazardous objects or areas that could cause injury. The coach can simply do this by walking the training area and looking for any problems. In outdoor facilities these may include broken glass, large stones, potholes or standing water. For an indoor area we may need to look at slippery surfaces, consider fire regulations and evacuation meeting points.

All the equipment being used during the training session should also be checked especially the goals.

What might be an issue or requirement when considering the goals being used?

The goals must be securely anchored to the ground. Portable goalposts must be either pinned or weighted to prevent them from toppling forward. Never let the players climb on, swing on or play with the structures of the goals. Under no circumstances should home made goalposts be used.

What else do you think the coach should have or do to maintain the health and safety of the players?

All the players and coaches taking part should have given the lead coach contact phone numbers in case of an emergency during the training period.

All the players and coaches should be informed as to where the nearest phone is. If the nearest phone is a mobile, does it need a pin number to activate it? This is in case you yourself are injured and someone else needs to make a call.

The coach should always have a medical kit on hand and the contents should be checked prior to any training session. The location of the medical kit should be known by all the players and coaches and be within easy reach.

The coach should be made aware if any of the players have a special medical condition. If specialist treatment (inhalers etc) is required then the player should make the coach aware of where the required medication is. Any medication should also be clearly labelled with the full name of the player.

The coach should check the attire and equipment of the players. In particular the type of footwear being worn, the state of the studs or blades and ensure the players are wearing shin pads. Have the players got the right clothing, is it warm enough for winter, waterproof or suitable for a hot summer day. The players should also remove any glasses or jewellery being worn and also remove any sweets or chewing gum.

Having looked into the health and safety issues both for our players and the facility we can now look at our session plan.

One of the most important requirements to being a good coach is preparation. The coach must know exactly what they are going to coach and how they are going to coach it. A coaching 'session plan' should be written out in advance and take into account a number of different issues.

Let's consider what needs to be prepared by the coach prior to any coaching session and list them?

Firstly where is the training facility? Are we using an indoor or outdoor area, what size area is it? How should it be organised?

How long will our coaching session last, one, two hours? How will the different parts of the session and the timings fit together? How long will we warm up? What about the drill or drills and how long will the game at the end last?

What about the equipment, does the coach need to bring the equipment or is it at the facility? How many balls, bibs and cones are available for use? Remember portable goalposts require more time to put up and take down so make allowances and arrive early.

Coaching the Coach

We have asked many times throughout the book about the players we are going to coach so what do you think are their requirements?

How many players are you going to be coaching, 8 or 20? Will they need outdoor boots or indoor trainers? Have they played before or are they complete novices? What age group or standard are they and therefore what drill should they be taught. What are we concentrating on coaching them? What are the key points we want to explain and coach?

As you can see there is a lot to think about so lets try and make the whole process of taking a training session easier.

If you have just been elected coach of an Under 8's team by a group of parents or you are an experienced coach the first thing we need is a register of players.

The register can be to keep records of who turns up each week and if needed who pays and owes for the session. We can also use it to list emergency contact names, numbers and any player's medical conditions.

Let's have a look at a simple register for an under 8's team.

Grassroots FC Under 8's			Date: 21-3-06	Ref: ① TRAINING DRIBBLING Location / Time LONDON 10:00 – 11:00
No	**Name**	**Here**	**Fees**	**Contact**	**Comments**
1	Jim P	✓	£1	123123	
2	Chris M	✓	£1	234234	
3	Sam W	✓	OWES	345345	HAS NEW CONTACT PHONE Nº MUMS MOBILE 210210
4	Pete H	✓	£1	456456	
5	Roger S	✓	£1	567567	
6	Mark W	✓	£1	678678	Asthma, inhaler labelled in his Man Utd boot bag
7	Paul S	✓	£1	789789	
8	Barry M	✓	£1	890890	
9	Rich S	✓	£1	098098	
10	George M	✓	£1	987987	Chris's Dad Collects George after training
11	David S	✗		876876	PHONED UP WILL BE OK FOR GAME ON SATURDAY.
12	James S	✓	OWES	765765	
13	Dean S	✓	£1	654654	
14	Roger W	✓	£1	543543	
15	Ian H	✓	£1	432432	
16	Charlie H	✗		321321	

We have listed all the players with their contact numbers and space for any comments. We have also given them all a squad number. This means we can allocate the same numbered shirt and shorts to them and make sure we get them returned at the end of the season or should they leave.

The pre-prepared register has been completed by hand on the day of the session. Everyone who attended has been ticked and a cross has been put next to those who missed the session along with any comments.

The coach has been able to easily add any 'fees' payments and who still owes. There are known comments about Mark's medical condition. We know Mark suffers from Asthma so we can check prior to the session that his inhaler is labelled and in his Manchester United boot bag. We can also see that Chris's Dad collects George after training.

On the day of the session we can see that Sam has given us a new emergency contact number, so it is noted in the comments and the register can be updated.

There is also a date and reference on the top of the register. This means we can collate the register with the session plan.

Now we have a register, which is easily completed, and ready for use. It addresses the health and safety issues for our players so now we can move onto our session plan.

Lets say we have been asked to undertake the training session on basic dribbling for Grassroots FC Under 8's team. As per our register there are 16 players in the squad and they are training Saturday morning at the local park. The session will last one hour. Being the excellent well-prepared coach you are you have all the equipment you could possible need stored away at home. We will refer to this book to determine our drills and what we are trying to coach.

Will we need a warm up?

Yes. We stated this right at the start of the book. So what will you do?

We will start with our basic 20x20 area and have the players jogging about without a ball. We can list our dynamic stretches, knees up, bum kicks, jumps, skipping etc.

As they are young we can introduce imagination and stimulate them into thinking. Get the players to pretend the 20x20 square is a Zoo. Ask them what animals are in the zoo? Can they act like a monkey and swing their arms about? Roar, pounce and run about like a tiger or Jump about like a kangaroo?

How about pretending they are all in the World Cup Final and they must score a goal to win. Hold up an imaginary ball and just pretend to throw it into the square. Can the players leap and head the imaginary ball, twist and shoot, volley and dive, and most importantly run around with their hands in the air screaming when they pretend to score.

Lets introduce a ball. We can now have all our players dribbling about in the same 20x20 square. Looking through another book of drills you come across a dribbling game, 'Killer' or 'King of the Ring' which you think could be used in the warm up. This is a dribbling game where all the players within the square have a ball and dribble it about. Neither they nor their ball are allowed outside the square. We then have a couple of players who do not have footballs; these are the 'killers'. The killers are let loose on the players in the square and they have to try and kick the balls of all the other players out of the square. The last players left in the square with their balls are the winners. The winners take on the role of 'killers' for the next game.

Now we have completed a warm up that fits into the session criteria, basic dribbling, we can move onto the drill itself.

What are we going to coach and how, think about the age of the players and their skill level?

As they are a new squad of Under 8's lets try and coach them into using both feet, we will also need a bit of fun.

What drill do you think we can use from the book?

Lets use Dribbling Drill 2 - Dribbling around cones. We have 16 young players in the squad so lets think about the organisation of the drill.

How would you organise the drill for your 16 under 8's?

Because they are young and they need lots of practice we will have the players standing at each end of the line of cones. We can have two lines of cones and four players at each end.

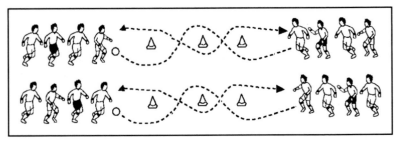

Remember from the register that when we turned up we had two players missing so we need to think on our feet and change the drill accordingly. What would be the easiest change?

Simply take away two players from the two lines on the right, one from each line.

So now we have a warm up and the organisation for our dribbling drill we can get on with coaching our players. We are trying to coach this group to use both feet so we need to concentrate on watching them doing the drill and correcting the mistakes. See page 10 to review the drill and coaching points. The particular extract is highlighted below.

Watch the younger players can you spot any problems?

A lot of younger players will try and run around the ball so they can kick it back in another direction using their favourite foot. As the coach can you promote the use of both feet?

Can we get them into using the instep of their right foot when they kick left and the instep of the left foot when they kick to the right?

Now we have our coaching points.

Remember these are younger players so we will need to put in a bit of fun to finish off the drill. What did we say earlier in the book that we could do?

Simple races with goals awarded for finishing first.

Hopefully now you can see how this book can be used to help you coach and educate your players. Hopefully you are already thinking about the possible mistakes that can be made with adding the pressure of a race.

Will you coach them, step in and demonstrate the correct way? Did they understand? How do you know?

So now we have a warm up, a drill and our coaching points aimed specifically at the age and skill level of the players we are coaching. We almost have our session planned we just need to finish off the session as normal with a game.

Remember the key to a good coach and a good session is preparation, so we need to collate all our ideas. Lets simplify our notes, listing our coaching points as bullet points and prepare our session plan.

Warm Up - 15 minutes

1.   Jumps, skips, knees up etc.
2.   Imaginary animals, monkeys, tigers and kangaroo.
3.   Imaginary world cup final
4.   Killer

Dribbling Drill - Dribbling Around Cones - 15 minutes
1.   Instep of their right foot when they kick left
2.   Instep of the left foot when they kick to the right
3.   Races

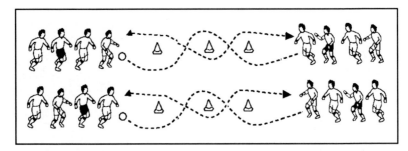

Game - 15 minutes

Each part of the session has 15-20 minutes allocated. The 15 minutes is for the drill and the extra 5 minutes will allow for drinks breaks, moving equiment, putting on bibs etc and talking about what has been coached.

Now we can move onto making sure we have all the equipment that we need to carry out our planned session.

What equipment do we need?

We need a set of cones, enough to mark out our 20x20 square, our dribbling drill and game. Our players need a ball each for dribbling and our 'Killer' warm up (16 balls). We also need a set of bibs and ideally a set of goals for the game.

Have we missed anything?

We should definitely have or know the location of a first aid bag and phone. We should also have a ball pump, stop watch and whistle.

We can now look at putting all these various parts together in one simple document, which is our session plan.

We need the date and reference number, this ties the register and session plan together. We will need to list the equipment requirements and duration of the session. The ability and the age of our players need to be included. Finally we need our brief notes and coaching points for the session.

Can you draw up a session plan for the Grassroots FC Under 8's training session on basic dribbling?

Coaching Session Plan

Group	Grassroots FC Under 8's		Session Date	21-3-06
Coach			Ref	7
Session Aim	Basic Dribbling – Dribbling Around Cones			
Duration	10:00 - 11:00	Age	New Under 8's	
No of Players	16	Ability	Beginners	
Equipment	First Aid Kit, mobile phone, 16 balls, Two sets of bibs, set of cones, ball pump, whistle.			

Session Plan   **Timings**

Session Plan	Timings
Warm Up: jumps, skips, knees up etc. Imaginary animals, monkeys, tigers and kangaroo. Imaginary world cup final. Dribbling around in square Killer	15 –20 Minutes
Main Content: Dribbling Round Cones – Add cones if too easy. **Coaching Points:** Instep of their right foot when they kick left Instep of the left foot when they kick to the right Races	15 – 20 minutes
Game: 60x40 pitch, 8 vs. 8.	15 – 20 minutes

This is a very easy and simple session plan based on a young group of inexperienced under 8's but how would you amend it for older or more experienced players. Obviously we need to pick more elaborate drills and maybe coach more points than just using both feet. Pick a drill from the book based on their skill level and add however many coaching points you feel they can absorb as a group.

CoachingtheCoach

The session plan is still done in the same way, select your warm up, drill and note the trigger words. Put in a diagram of your drill and the coaching points you want to elaborate upon. Finally add the game, maybe you will try a wing or third's game. Maybe you want to pick a drill from another book and use that. Just make sure the drill you pick can be used to coach the points you need. Note down the trigger words or coaching points in your session plan.

Lets really test ourselves and take a quick look at a squad of 16 Under 14's players which you need to coach. The manager is complaining that the team lose the ball too easily when the midfield is congested and there is no space to play.

Think about the problems, what will we coach and how?

This must seem very daunting but let us just simplify it again. If the team is losing the ball in a compact situation we need to create the same in training so they can experience it and improve. We need to build a session based on close control, finding space in a confined area and passing to the player in space. There are a number of drills in this book that can help, have a look through and see if you can pick any out.

Firstly there is Dribbling Drill 5 - Confined Space Dribbling. The problem our team has though is more to do with defenders and looking for the pass to a player in space.

Passing 2 - Passing 3 vs. 1 could be used and by making the square smaller we can create a more compact environment.

Passing 4 - Passing Team Challenge. We will use this drill because we can coach the whole squad. It can also be used to coach all the coaching points of the other drills.

What about the warm up?

Can we use Dribbling Drill 5 - Confined Space Dribbling as part of the warm up?

Yes, this will certainly prepare their control for the confined space of the main drill. We will also add some turns and explain about turning out of a tight area and into space.

What about the game?

Lets try a game of thirds where we have lots of players competing in midfield. This way we can see how successful our coaching was and how much the squad have progressed. So now lets put together a quick session plan.

Coaching Session Plan

Group	Grassroots FC Under 14's		Session Date	12-6-06
Coach			Ref	9
Session Aim	Improving control and passing within a compact area			
Duration	7:30 – 8:30	Age		Under 14's
No of Players	16	Ability		Very good
Equipment	First Aid Kit, mobile phone, 16 balls, Two sets of bibs, set of cones, ball pump, whistle.			

Session Plan	Timings
Warm Up: 20x20 square jumps, skips, knees up etc. Ball each dribbling lots of turns drag back, inside and outside hook. Confined Space Dribbling 4x4 square 8 working 8 resting.	15-20 Minutes
Main Content: Passing team Challenge **Coaching Points:** Within Confined Area Passing – short accurate, weight. Receiving skills - Open your body up to see the whole area Support – Can you receive the ball? Decision – Pass or hold Disguise – Fake to pass or turn Dribbling – keep hold of the ball Outer Area Create Space – Where is the space Passing – Long lofted into space 7 v 3 in middle 6 in outer area - coach passing and holding the ball.	15-20 minutes
Game: Thirds game on a 60x40 pitch, 8 vs. 8. both playing 2,4,2 formation	15-20 minutes

Now we have looked at a problem in a game and used the book to prepare a session to help our players improve. Could you make up a session plan for an under 12's team who want to be taught some turns? How about an Under 9's team who want to head the ball? Could you now make up a session plan to improve an under 10's team which is having problems scoring goals in and around the penalty box?

What else might you want to include as you continue to coach?

It would be easy to add comments on the session plan about your players performances and indeed your own. How did your coaching affect the players? Did you demonstrate or were you just talking? Did you question your players? Would you change anything? Did the players find the drill too easy or too difficult? Did they understand? How would this affect your next session? Based on the player's strengths and weaknesses what will be your next session?

Remember to ask for feedback from the players was there anything they particularly liked or found dull and boring. Use their input to improve your sessions and coaching.

Lets go back to the original Grassroots FC under 8's Basic Dribbling session we did earlier. Imagine how it went. They were inexperienced under 8's but picked up on using both feet very quickly. During the session we remembered from the book that we could progress the drill. We added only the inside and outside of the left foot then only the inside and outside of the right foot. What about explaining the drill to the players? They did not understand our long rambling explanation but as soon as we demonstrated it was all clear.

Looking back on this session what might you do to change or improve the session and your coaching?

We will add progressions to our coaching points making sure we have enough to coach. We will think about demonstrating more and talking less especially with younger players. Make a note of your performance so you can analyse it over a number of weeks. Use the simple evaluation form, which you can add to the back of your session plan and have everything in one place.

Let us look at a simple self evaluation sheet for the session with Grassroots FC under 8's we have just discussed.

Group	Grassroots FC Under 8's	Session Date	21-3-06
Coach		Ref	7

Was the session content in line with the player's age and skill level?	DRILL MADE IT EASY TO COACH WHAT I WANTED
Were the arrangements and organisation ok? I.e. the health and safety, equipment, facility	YES
Was the coaching technique and communication appropriate?	NO - TOO MUCH TALKING NEED TO DEMONSTRATE THEN LET THEM TRY.
Were any Changes made to the session?	YES, EXTRA COACHING POINTS ADDED DRIBBLING WITH 1 FOOT ONLY . LEFT THEN RIGHT
Did the players improve?	YES
Did you get any feedback?	PLAYERS ENJOYED THE SESSION ESPECIALLY RACES AND KILLER
If you did this session again what would you change?	BE QUICKER STOP TALKING DEMO AND MOVE ON, ADD MORE COACHING POINT TO PLAN.

Can you learn from this evaluation sheet when planning your next session?

Yes

We have moved back to improving ourselves as a coach again. We are using the session plan and self evaluation forms and thinking about our performance as a coach, and the performances of our players. We are evaluating ourselves, learning and improving based on our experiences. We are improving on the things that work and learning from the things that don't. We can evaluate new drills to see if they work and if they can be used again. We can see which drills and coaching points go together in order to improve our players.

Now we are improving as a coach.

Now we are affecting our players

Now we are coaching.

Summary

I have a lot of coaches asking what the FA Level 2 course entails and how it differs so much from the Level 1 course.

This book has given you an insight into those differences. Why do we coach certain things, what are they and how do we coach them.

We have moved on from simply selecting drills and supervising. We are watching our players and looking for mistakes. We know why they make the mistake. We can question our players, do they understand and if they don't we can explain why, and show them. We are challenging our players to try something harder or with their weaker foot. We are thinking about our players and how we can positively affect and improve them. We are thinking about our own performance. Analysing what was good and how we can improve what was not so good.

I hope this book has shown you that logical thought and knowledge of key points are invaluable in the education of our players.

Expand your knowledge and take the FA Coaching Courses. Watch qualified and experienced coaches. Ask them to give you feedback on your own sessions. Improve yourself and improve your players.

For more information on the Level 2 Certificate in Coaching Football, you can visit www.1st4sportqualifications.com

Good Luck

The Association of Football Coaches

"Helping the coaches and teachers of today to produce the players and teams of tomorrow"

What is it?

It is an independent association, fully supported by PUMA consisting of coaches of all abilities who are involved in the coaching of football to players of all levels, ages and gender.

Who are its members?

Anyone can join the scheme as it is not restricted to coaches with previous qualifications. Therefore membership is open to everyone including teachers, youth team coaches, managers and all those individuals coaching football.

Peter Crouch -
"There is nothing like this in the football industry at the moment and it provides a wonderful opportunity for all coaches at all levels."

JOIN NOW!

You, too, can then enjoy the benefits of being a member of The Coaches Association:-

• Unique membership number allowing you to explore the 'members only' site, enter competitions, attend events and download drills from top class coaches
• Free gift on signing up
• Discretionary prices on products
• Access to professional players and coaches
• Contact with a whole host of other members who share your common interest, plus so much more

www.thecoachesassociation.com
Tel: 0844 8001825

Lightning Source UK Ltd.
Milton Keynes UK
20 November 2009

146510UK00002B/35/P

9 780755 210749